CONTENTS

Bonus Chapters

This book is a guide for someone who is incarcerated or facing imprisonment. It doesn't take a degree in quantum physics to figure out that putting people in prison is big business in America. If every law that was written was always obeyed then apparently someone would be out of a job. Lawyers, judges, probation officers, correctional officers, etc…the list goes on and on. What if you ran the judicial system in America, making billions of dollars? Would you design your system for prisoners to be rehabilitated, or would you set your system up so that those prisoners remained uneducated almost guaranteeing his or her returning for a second or third sentence?

Now I'm not saying get rid of all prisons and let the criminal element run free. Please don't think that. I have been in prison myself and I know a few people who should never be allowed out of prison. I will also say that I have witnessed a few prisoners educate themselves because failure was not an option for them.

What is my point? Okay, maybe we need a balance in the way this whole incarceration process is handled on a larger scale. Let's just say for example that you are sitting behind bars right now reading this book or maybe you are free but have a loved one in prison. One of the key questions you might ask yourself is 'why did I commit that crime?' or 'how did my son, daughter, husband, or wife end up in prison?' Then your next thought is, 'I know I'm smarter that that,' or 'I know he or she is smarter than that.' Well, maybe you are but with all due respect please allow me to give you a reality check. If you were smarter than that you probably wouldn't be in prison right now. I hate to be so raw, but it's true. Educate yourself now!

What if you had a chance to attend one of the best colleges in America and get a degree along with a good job? I'm not saying that people with college degrees never go to prison, but there are fewer people in prison with college degrees compared to high school dropouts. Okay, you made some poor choices in life that landed yourself in prison. The good news is that it's not over.

You might have two years or ten. Maybe you have a life sentence. The purpose for me writing this book is to give you a blueprint to take and create a program that will make your prison time easier to handle. This book will give you insight on how to enhance your education and provide thinking strategies that troubleshoot problems that might occur during your prison term. This book should only be viewed as a tool to get your mind on the right track. You have to do the driving. I can only provide the roadmap.

Thou Shalt Overcome Depression, Anger, and Stress

Okay, this is your first year behind the iron curtain and you really need to get your emotions in tact. There are prisoners around you all day. Some of them are laughing and joking. It seems like everybody is in a good mood except you and a few others that rode on the bus with you. Never mind lifting weights, you would rather eat a few oatmeal cakes and crawl on your bunk. Not to mention that the whole place is disgusting. The toilets have no boarders around them. Four men take showers at the same time in the same shower. Plus the food is horrible.

All of these circumstances can lead to depression, anger, and stress. I can help you get rid of depression, anger and stress but before you can get rid of something you have to understand the origin of it.

DEPRESSION

Depression is an emotional disorder marked by an inability to concentrate, insomnia, and feelings of guilt and dejection. Being able to concentrate is having the ability to focus on something. Most people experience some form of depression when they enter prison because there is so much noise and movement around them that they lose focus on themselves. Feelings of guilt may cause you to overeat. These negative emotions can cause you to sleep during the day and stay up all night which can lead to insomnia. The good news is that your depression is a natural emotion due to the circumstances around you and in time it will fade away.

If you don't believe me, just look at the old man/woman in your block. He/she may have been in prison since the eighties but they still manage to laugh and smile. 'Why is that?' you might ask yourself. That older person can smile because he/she has the ability to focus again. You can do the same thing. There are many different techniques that you can use to get your concentration back on track. Reading is probably the best way to focus. Just go to the library and check out books that interest you. Reading is a very positive way to educate yourself and consume time all in one. (Refer to Chapter 9). Word searches and crossword puzzles are excellent choices too. Not only do they consume time but they enhance your vocabulary. Always keep a crossword or word search book with you in the event that you are placed in segregation. You will be grateful that you did.

Reading is also an excellent way to be near and far at the same time, meaning you can have your eyes in your book but your ears should be listening to what the other prisoners are talking about. Then you can determine who is good and who is evil. People say the craziest things when they think no one is listening.

Card and board games are fine but this involves a little too much interacting with people who may try to leech off of you later on. I strongly recommend that you do not play any games during your first year or at least until you have a complete program that balances your mental and physical activities.

Weightlifting and physical fitness is also a good way to overcome depression and insomnia. Believe me, if you work out for two hours a day every Monday through Thursday then insomnia probably won't be a problem for you. (Refer to Chapter Five for more information on physical fitness.)

ANGER

Anger is a feeling of great displeasure and hostility according to Webster's Dictionary. These emotions are self explanatory. Your displeasure comes from your own surroundings of course. You show me someone who enjoys being incarcerated and I'll show you a fool. The truth is that displeasure and hostility are cousins. When you spot one of them that means the other one is close by. One might ask, 'what is the cure for displeasure and hostility?' Unfortunately displeasure and hostility is always alive in prison but there are a few simple things you can do to add a little comfort during your stay in prison…

   A) Pay someone in the clothes house to give you new t-shirts, boxers, pants, shirts, and socks.

(Officers treat you better when your clothes are neat and clean.)

B) Pay someone in the kitchen to give you extra food during chowtime. (Walking around hungry causes hostility.)

C) Manage your money wisely. If you spend more than three dollars a day, then you are over spending.

D) If you are fortunate enough to have someone on the outside to send you money on a regular basis, please keep the information to yourself. Never brag.

STRESS

Stress is strain or a force that deforms. Stress is mental or physical tension. Tension is force that pulls negative emotions from your inner being. Stress is also known as the silent killer. Too much stress can cause high blood pressure, stomach ulcers and/or heart disease.

Prison is a stressful place altogether. You have to deal with multiple personalities everyday. How you handle stress determines your health physically and mentally. Here are a few ways to cope with stress...

A) Exercise three to five days a week. (Refer to Chapter Five.)

B) Join a support group like Alcoholics Anonymous or Narcotics Anonymous and attend religious services.

C) Watch TV sitcom shows. (Laughter is always good medicine.)

D) Communicate with your family whenever possible (if this is possible.)

Once you learn how to master depression, anger, and stress everything else is a piece of cake. What makes these three killers so difficult to handle is that they are initially a part of you in the first stage of your incarceration. The good news is that you can beat depression and stress. It may not be a swift defeat but if you follow these guidelines you will definitely make things better for yourself.

Albert Einstein said, "reality is merely and illusion albeit a very persistent one." I know your situation is very real but you must realize that you have the ability to alter your reality by having a positive mental attitude (PMA). Thinking and acting in a positive manner will attract positive people and things into your life.

Don't expect to change overnight. Your success depends on your ability to focus on yourself. I know you probably feel hurt and rejected. I have been in your situation before and the best thing you can do is accept it for what it is and move on. This too shall pass.

2

Thou Shalt Understand the Different Inmate Personalities

The Wannabee

The wannabee inmate is that guy who is always lying or cheating just to fit in or be cool. He/she is not focused on rehabilitating themselves at all, but would rather stick his/her nose in somebody else's business just to stir confusion.

It's easy to spot a wannabee because they are always in somebody's face seeking entertainment through falsehoods and he said-she said stories. The wannabee will go to any length to befriend a new inmate. Understand that the wannabee's sole purpose is to get information from people so that he/she can twist the story and pass it on to others for a quick laugh or two.

A wannabee will offer you items such as food or coffee as a play to engage in conversation with you. I would advise you to stay away from this shady character unless you want your business all over the yard. If you are approached by the wannabee don't become hostile. Speak if you are spoken to but never give out any of your personal information. You can run him/her away by flipping the script and asking them about their intentions towards you or just asking them personal questions about him/herself. Nine times out of ten the wannabee will become uncomfortable with your questions and find a way to get away from you. Never show a wannabee your family pictures.

ALPHA MALE

The alpha male is usually the guy who runs everything from the card games to the commissary/canteen. He is usually the dude with the muscles. He spends a lot of time lifting weights. He also studies and reads a lot of books. He is sharp physically and mentally.

He probably won't say anything to you when he sees you but be assured that he is watching everything you do. A female can also be an alpha. An alpha is usually a good person with a standard of morals and ethics. Some leaders in prison usually have a group of people that help them enforce their rules, but an alpha male/female is the type of person that usually stands alone when he/she imposes his rules on another.

Most of the rules that an alpha imposes are for the good of everyone else. He/she is very intelligent and can become easily agitated in the presence of a wannabee or a bully. The best way to deal with an alpha is to stay out of his/her face. An alpha will usually have respect for someone that listens instead of running off at the mouth. It's cool to speak to an alpha but you can also agitate him/

her by speaking to them numerous times in one day. If an alpha tried to impose a rule on you that you don't agree with calmly stand your ground and don't back down. He/ she will have no choice but to respect you and you will also gain respect with others. Use sound judgment when standing your ground because a good reputation goes far in prison.

Punks, Undercover Punks

A punk is a guy who walks and talks like a female. He has decided that life would be easier for him if he acts like a female. The strange thing is that he is right. The staff, correctional officers, and most inmates show the punk much respect. Most punks have female names and some even have breasts. Punks style their hair in women's fashions and wear perfume. If he is attracted to you then he will watch you and look for signs of you being attracted to him. The slightest signal you give (extended eye contact) will be viewed as an attraction to him. He will make a move towards you if he is confident about your signals. Some female correctional officers will tell a punk to try and get close to you just to learn if you are gay or not. If you decide to fall for the setup, then plan to have your business all over the prison. My sincere advice to you is to keep your distance from the punk. It's okay to speak to them but it's even better to return to your family safe and one hundred percent healthy.

Undercover Punks...

These guys are tricky because they talk and look like normal men. Some of them even profess to be killers. I would hate to alarm you but undercover punks make up about 60% of the prison population. Most of them seem to be masculine and they always comment on women's backsides. It is easy to spot an undercover punk if you just pay attention. Most undercover punks will call the punks by their female name and hold two and three hour conversations with them.

Most of them are very unintelligent and they enjoy watching television all day. These men and I use the word men loosely) tend to lean more towards fiction than fact. For example, instead of watching the world news he may want to see The Simpsons. Undercover punks always talk about their sexual encounters with women to other men for arousal. Don't indulge in those conversations about your sexual encounters because it is merely a setup. The first time one of these perverts try to engage in a dialogue about their sexual encounters tell him that you don't want to hear about it. If he asks you why, don't answer. Don't move and look him straight in the eye. If he begins to talk just walk away and leave him looking like a babbling idiot. You do not want to mistakenly become friends with an undercover punk. That's like befriending a CIA agent. Remember reputation is everything. Stay healthy.

COWARD

Cowards come in all shapes and sizes. Some of them have big mouths that they use to try and intimidate others. They are very emotional for example. If they lose a basketball game they might get upset and throw the basketball over the fence. Most of them don't want to fight or have any type of physical confrontation. They run their mouths because they think the loud noise will scare people away.

Most cowards fear confrontation and will go to any length to avoid it. On the flip side he/she will get involved with gossip. Cowards always need to know what happened, when it happened, and why because they are afraid the same will happen to them.

When a coward makes an attempt to bring you in his/her world of gossip just let him/her know politely that you don't talk about people and you make it a point to mind your business. A coward will always attempt to deceive you. For example, if you are asleep and miss breakfast a coward will lie and tell you that he tried to awaken you. Stay on point.

THE SNITCH

A snitch used to be considered a low down, dirty rat at one time. These days snitching is used as an offense for someone who needs to score. When I use the word score it means to win. Snitches don't want to do any more than they have to. They win by getting their time reduced or completely dismissed. Snitches are always looking for a way to lighten their sentence and they cooperate with the correctional officers one hundred percent. I once heard a correctional officer say that snitched make her job so easy. Snitches understand that they are living in the information era, so when they get in trouble they just give the authorities information about the conduct and behavior of other inmates in exchange for a slap on the hand.

You can always spot a snitch by paying close attention. A snitch is always walking around, looking and investigating something or somebody. They almost always need approval from a correctional officer. A snitch will always try to entertain an officer with either tall tales or comedy routines. I would tell you to stay away from a snitch but that would be virtually impossible because they are everywhere.

When you encounter a snitch do not become hostile with him/her. He/she is another set of eyes for the staff. Try to be on your best behavior so that the snitch will give the authorities a good report concerning you. If you are hostile towards a snitch he will give a bad report on your behavior to the police anyway. This might haunt you in the future.

The Conman

The conman is an inmate who is always trying to get over on someone. He/she will lie about any and everything. He/she will tell you that they are wealthy and own mansions and expensive cars. Most of the time they have nothing. A conman's purpose is to convince you that they have it all so you will feel comfortable when he/she asks you for some cosmetics to gamble with. The majority of a conman's sentence is spent at the gambling table. If he loses at the table he will call his wife or mother and tell her that he needs money for a college training course or a lie similar to that. If he/she can't get the money from his/her family then he/she will prey on individuals they consider to be weak. You can spot a conman before he spots you. He/she is the person you see looking in your locker when you have it open. The conman will do a quick fifteen second scan of everything in your locker. He/she will make a mental note of any items they can use at the gambling table. A few days later the conman will ask you if you have any soap, lotion, or shampoo that he can borrow. He/she already knows that you have it. Their purpose is to see if you are an easy target. Don't take it personally and never give him anything. A conman will ask certain people in his family to send pictures of their cars and houses only to lie and say those things belong to him/her. The sad part about this is that the conman actually believes that he/she is doing the right thing. You can throw anybody off their mark if they assume you are a target. This is done by making yourself seem near when you are far and far when you are near them. Example: If you are in a closed area (a dormitory at night) and people are gathered around in groups talking in your presence, they probably are checking you out in a discreet way. You have become a target. Distance yourself from the group by reading a book or writing a letter. If you own a walkman radio or an IPod, place the ear phones in your ears but listen to the conversations around you. Remember, a person will reveal a lot about themselves when they think no one is paying attention. This is how you make yourself far when you are near. The reversal of this is making yourself near when you are far. Example: If you think someone may be targeting you for whatever reasons then you need to throw him/her off your scent. You can make yourself seem near when you are far by watching the person who is watching you. Do this when you are preoccupied at that particular moment. You can watch them when he/she is playing sports (basketball or volleyball) or when they are playing cards or chess. This tactic will subconsciously let your opponent know that you are watching them watch you.

Thief

The thief is not really a problem in prison believe it or

not. It's kind of difficult to steal when you are around hundreds of people at a time. If somebody steals from you, nine times out of ten the snitch will tell you who it was. Snitches are everywhere at all times. Plus you have the officers who walk around. Don't forget about the alpha male. He does not tolerate a thief at any expense. Most inmates despise a thief and will usually unite to get rid of one. If someone steals from you it's not the end of the world. You don't have to fight him/her. Just let everyone know who the thief is and they will get rid of him/her. A thief hates to be exposed.

CLOWN

This guy is good to have around for entertainment but he can be facetious at times. He/she is constantly seeking attention and if you are not careful they might try to make you a part of their comedy act. A clown is also considered to be a person who uses poor judgment when making decisions. For example, someone who decides to smoke marijuana a day before the guards round up inmates for urine analysis tests and ends up with a dirty urine sample is usually referred to as a clown. He/she feels like it's his/her duty to make everyone laugh. Laughter can definitely be a good thing in prison if people are laughing with you. You might have a problem when people are laughing at you. If you end up being the butt of a clown's jokes there are two ways to deal with this situation. The first way is to ignore the clown and show no emotion at all. The second way is to laugh at the clown just to throw him off by revealing to everyone that you don't take yourself too seriously. You can also use both of these techniques from time to time just to make it difficult for the clown to figure you out. Remember, if a person can't figure you out that means they have to approach you with caution.

BULLY

The bully is related to the coward because they basically have the same characteristics. The bully is a little louder and more aggressive than the coward. He/she will attempt to start you down. You must always make strong eye contact with a bully and never lower your eyes. If he/she thinks you are intimidated by their looks then you will have a problem. When you engage in a standoff with a bully he/she might ask you why you are looking at them. Don't say anything because they are trying to set you up. Continue to stare him/her down until they call you crazy and walk away. Congratulations, you just called the bully's bluff. A bully will also test you by placing his/her hand on your shoulder when they first meet you. Tell him/her politely that you only allow your family members to touch you. If a stranger puts his hands on you then he is violating your personal space which is a sign of disrespect. Never allow a bully to raise his voice or curse at you. Stand your ground. Every man feels some type of fear when they are confronted by someone. A bully is also afraid.

MR. INSTITUTIONALIZED

This guy suffers from an identity crisis and has a personality disorder. He/she will usually have a trace of some of the other personalities previously stated. Mr. Institutionalized is petty by nature. He/she is mentally weak and has more than likely done a lot of prison time. Things that appear small to the average person are huge to him/her. Example: You may have just finished eating your lunch but you left a slice of bread on your tray. Mr. Institutionalized will think that you are wasting state money by throwing the slice of bread in the trash. He/she will most likely become emotional when watching television and talk to the television as if the characters can hear him/her. He/she will usually be the first to wake up in the morning, dressed and ready for work. If someone borrows and item from Mr. Institutionalized and doesn't give it back he will become highly upset and emotional. He/she views other inmates as subordinates and places himself on the authoritative level as the officers. Yes, Mr. Institutionalized is usually a snitch.

3

Thou Shalt Understand Male Correctional Officers

Most male correctional officers are laid back guys who just want to mind their business and get a check every two weeks. There are a few of them who get off on making you miserable. You have to be cautious with these officers because some of them wear masks. They will be somewhat friendly towards you during your initial confrontations with them. They do this to get personal information from you. This information is used to determine whether or not you will become a target for verbal or possibly physical abuse later on. You also have to understand that some of these officers have been working in prisons for ten years or longer and they are also institutionalized. They posses the same personality traits discussed in chapter two. Please don't be alarmed when I use the term physical abuse. Most male correctional officers are not trying to fight anyone, but there are a few who would enjoy getting in an argument with you so they can slap handcuffs on you and take you to segregation. They don't want to hurt you but if you get out of line and one of the officers kicks you in the butt on your way to the hole, let's just say it makes good conversation in the officers' lunch room the next day.

The average male correctional officer spends most of his time trying to prove that he is 'cool' to the inmates but stern around his superiors. He can get away with this very easily because there is a very thin line between officer and inmate these days. Inmates act like officers and vice versa. I have even witnessed an inmate make rounds every thirty minutes like an officer does.

Some of these correctional officers are former military personnel and ex-police officers. Those are the ones who carry chips on their shoulders all the time. You can usually spot one of these officers by his movement. He will try to stare you down at some point. He will use this tactic to see if you are intimidated. If you lower your eyes or drop your head he will think you are a punk or you are doing something that goes against D.O.C. policy.

Either way you are a target now. This anal retentive officer will put you under a microscope. Your locker will be searched whenever he is working. He may even pull you off the yard for a strip search. If you are gay then the two of you will enjoy the search, but if you are straight then you will be ready to lose it. To avoid this harassment all you need to do is look this officer straight in the eyes and tell him that he does not intimidate you. He's going to tell you that he's not trying to intimidate you and that he's just doing his job. Yes, he is doing his job but there is a reason that he chose you out of everyone else. That's when you politely let him know that he has you confused with someone else. The officer will begin asking questions like, 'Where are you from?' Don't answer him. Let him become a babbling idiot while you remain silent. (Make sure you follow his orders.) You won't have to worry about this guy again. He might say something every now and then but that's as far as he will go. Don't be afraid to express yourself around correctional officers. Remember to follow the rules and try not to use profanity.

Don't be naïve. There are some male correctional officers who are gay. They might not show it or prance around but there are signs to look for. The first sign is long periods of eye contact. If the officer looks at you longer than ten seconds then he might be gay. The second sign is his approach. The officer is always approaching you when no one is around. He seems to take a personal interest in you. He is either gay or he might think you are a snitch and is trying to recruit you. Don't snap at him right away. See what his angle is because some officers are religious men who win souls back to Christ. If this is the case then you may want to listen, but if the officer is some kind of freak then you need to tell him to get away from you. (Refer to undercover punk in Chapter 2.) If he is looking for a snitch and if you are one, it's show time, but if you're not tell the officer to keep it moving.

The third sign is the strip search. Most heterosexual officers hate strip searching male prisoners for obvious reasons. They want to get it over with just as much as you do. The most they will do is ask you to pull your boxers down to your knees, squat, and cough. The gay correctional officer will ask you to grab your cheeks and pull them apart. This is when you have to let him know in a very loud tone that you don't play those gay games and he should find somebody else to play with. Whatever you do don't grab your butt cheeks. You can drop your boxers and squat but don't follow his rule. Don't worry about a write-up because what officer in his right mind would write a man up for not grabbing his butt cheeks?

I can't forget about those high ranking male correctional officers. These guys walk around with titles like lieutenant and captain. Most of them have been officers for fifteen and twenty years. As long as you stay out of trouble these officers don't care what you do. When your name is constantly coming up then you are a problem. These guys walk around like they are gods in the flesh. The truth is that you probably wouldn't be able to recognize them without the uniform. Most of these officers become so self absorbed that they begin to treat the officers under them like inmates.

You can't talk to these officers like you would a regular officer. A high ranking officer has zero tolerance for backtalk. The only thing you can do to earn a high ranking officer's respect is by going over his command. If you have been mistreated by a high ranking officer don't hesitate to write a complaint or write the regional office in your area. You can also have your family members contact the high ranking officer and address the problem. If it's one thing a high ranking officer fears it's an inmate's family that loves and supports him/her. That leaves him responsible for your well being.

Don't be fooled by the high ranking officer's tough guy antics. He has been on the job for years and he probably has taken a beating by an inmate at one point or another. I'm not telling you to power drive him into the wall if he disrespects you. My point is that most of these guys (high ranking officers) are really insecure and afraid of what might happen to them so they put on the tough guy act. Don't let it intimidate you, but it's probably a good idea to stay out of his way.

The best way to deal with male correctional officers is to distance yourself from them. It's kind of ironic that they are called correctional officers because many of them would make lousy role models. You very seldom see a male correctional officer in good physical condition. These guys sit around all day at work and at home. If you don't believe me just ask an officer what he did last weekend. More than likely he will say that he sat around his house drinking the whole time. I don't mean to degrade male correctional officers because there are a few who have themselves together. These officers are usually between forty-five and fifty years old. They are very religious and dedicated to their families. You can get good advice from these types of officers because they stay the same way all the time. He won't compromise his beliefs or values for the captain or an inmate. If he sees another officer mishandling an inmate he won't hesitate to stand up for the inmate.

Be aware of the officer who is always smiling and telling jokes on inmates. He is a male gossip and nobody's business is safe around him. He would talk about your mother if he knew her. His fellow co-workers confide in him with certain issues and he informs the inmates about the private lives of his co-workers. Then he turns around and does the same thing to the inmates. Some people find him amusing but all he's doing is creating tension in an already tense environment. I remember being around a big mouth officer like this in 2004. He told a few inmates about his sexual encounters that he had with a female correctional officer. The conversation that he had with the inmates got back to her, and she was so upset that she shot him in the parking lot the next day. He lived and of course she was charged but I feel like he kind of had that coming to him. Remember pressure busts pipes. If you think the male gossip is bad just multiply his actions by ten and you have your female correctional officer. (Refer to Chapter 4.)

The male gossip is also similar to the wannabee (refer to Chapter 2). His biggest problem is boredom and he creates chaos for his entertainment purposes only. Stay away from this idiot because he's similar to an airplane that ran out of fuel at sixty thousand feet. Yes, he's about to crash. Don't go down with him. Guys like him never accomplish much in life because they can't keep their mouth shut. The captain and lieutenant won't promote him because they are afraid that he will put their business out in the open. The male gossip is a buffoon on the road to nowhere.

Staying out of people's business is the golden rule in prison. This is an excellent way to keep stitches out of your head. Don't get caught up in prison politics. Believe nothing that you hear and everything you see. This applies to officers and inmates. The only difference between the officer and inmate is that the officer gets to go home everyday. People are people no matter where you are. Your time should be spent on educating yourself and not what car officer Jones is driving.

Stay focused on yourself because you need to figure out what's wrong with you. If everything was all good with you then you wouldn't be in prison. I know there are some innocent people in prison and my heart goes out to you. If you are innocent then I would suggest you do some deep soul searching and seek spiritual guidance before this time makes you coldhearted and bitter. Prison is a cancer that eats away at your soul. You have to be strong because at this point in life failure shouldn't be an option for you. Truthfully this is the lowest point a person can go without dying. All you can do is work your way back on top.

Try not to take the officer's words and actions offensively. You will understand in due time why he acts that way. Most of the inmates around you are very manipulative and always trying to run some type of game on someone. Being a correctional officer puts you in the situation where you see the same stupid games being played over and over again. If you saw the same thing over and over again you would eventually get tired of it. The next step is losing interest in the people that run the games. You shouldn't be upset if an officer talks to you as if you were a fool. Politely let the officer know that he has no reason to talk to you in that manner (unless you are a fool). He might not show it that particular moment but he will make a mental note of what you say and he will slowly start showing you a little respect when he sees you. Respect is something you have to earn in prison. You can say who you are but nobody cares. Lead by example and people will follow you.

Don't talk about it, be about it. You can make yourself a better person in time. Never be afraid to notice your weaknesses. You can't become a stronger person if you can't know your weakness. If you do something wrong, don't beat yourself up. Lay on your bunk and figure out what you did wrong and create a way to stop doing it.

Remember don't believe anything people tell you, no matter how good it may sound. Pick up books and study for yourself.

4

Thou Shalt Never Understand Female Correctional Officers

If you could talk to some of my friends they will tell you that women are one of my favorite subjects. I find women to be complex, sexy, but emotional spirits. How the creator could place so much beauty in one creature is something I'll never understand. I love women and I spend a lot of time thinking of ways to make the women in my life extremely happy. One of the greatest things that I have ever witnessed in my lifetime is having a woman smile at me for no apparent reason. I know that might sound a little crazy but doing prison time will give you a greater appreciation of women.

What happens when you put a uniform on a lady and place her in charge of hundreds of men? I'll tell you what happens. You will have hundreds of men acting like complete idiots. I had the pleasure of interviewing a female correctional office who worked at a women's prison and she told me that the female prisoners show more aggressive signs of attraction to the female officers than most men. A female in uniform is equal to a superhero like Wonder Woman or Superwoman.

You probably won't believe the power these female officers possess. I'm not just talking about physical power, but they also have great mental powers once they learn how to use them. Imagine yourself as a prison guard surrounded by the opposite sex and every two minutes someone would tell you how good you look or how much they have been thinking of you. Do you know what this would do to your ego? Please don't get it confused. Some of those female officers are butt ugly inside and outside. These women are showered with so much praise and attention from the inmates that they actually believe what they are being told. Some inmates will literally fight one another for the officer's attention. Then you have those inmates who want to save the lady officer. Yes, I mean save as in talking to her about religion, life, or they will secretly offer her physical protection against rebellious inmates. All of this attention will blow her head up and she will come to the conclusion that she is god's gift to man. In a strange way she is god's gift to man for eight hours a day anyway.

The reversal to this situation is the drop dead gorgeous female officer. I have seen a few female officers that looked like supermodels. These women will make a man's jaw hit the floor. When they start working for D.O.C., in the beginning stages the high ranking officer watches the beauty like a hawk. He won't even let her too far out of his eyesight for obvious reasons. The high ranking male officer will assign her to a less stressful job like working in the control tower or the nurses' station. He shields her from the population.

He doesn't want her to quit so he almost immediately promises her a high ranking position with perks. Once he sees progress in her work his next step is to train her to hate inmates. The high ranking male officer will inform her of every dirty, filthy, disgusting activity that takes place in the prison population. Any time the female beauty is away from the high ranking officer he will assign at least two male officers to assist and escort her in the prison. Imagine what's going through her mind at that moment. She figures it out. All she has to do is treat the inmates and most of her coworkers like trash and she will continue receiving the royal treatment. She has no idea that the high ranking male officer will be running her life outside of work as well. She will grow tired of this game after a few years and become very bitter with herself and the job. She won't take her frustrations out on the high ranking officer because he is her meal ticket but everyone else will feel her scorn, especially you.

You can greet her with a hello but anything more than that is asking for trouble. If you tell her she is pretty don't be surprised if she handcuffs you and places you in segregation. Any compliment you give her will only embarrass her. She will spare you if you ignore her. Show this goddess too much attention and she will take it as a sign of disrespect. Remember the old saying, 'Never look a gift horse in the mouth.' The difference between the regular female officer and the supermodel officer is that the regular one craves your attention, because when she is at home and has no need to wear a uniform she hardly gets any attention. Her outside of prison world sucks because she becomes institutionalized and starts running stupid prison games on men in the real world. They view her as crazy and leave her alone. The gorgeous female officer knows she is pretty and can live without your attention. She would rather be in an abusive relationship that makes her feel like a regular human being. Just like a superhero, their powers are in the uniform.

I can't forget about the cougar female officer. If you are an inmate over thirty years old she doesn't want you. She is attracted to younger inmates and will give them special attention. This lady is between forty and sixty years old and very attractive for an older lady. The older inmates think that she should be hanging out with them so they get frustrated with her fraternization with the younger crowd. What makes the older crowd even more upset is that when a female officer ignores one of them he/she will find something that might not be so appealing about the female officer (overweight, bad skin, big feet…) and crack jokes about her, but the cougar female officer very seldomly has any visible flaws. If she does and one of the inmates attempts to expose her she will flip the scenario and have everybody laughing at him/her because her years of imprisonment gave her a smart mouth and a swift tongue. The cougar female officer has already sized you up and she is prepared to make a fool out of you if you rub her the wrong way. This lady is very smart. The younger guys love her because unlike most of the officers she is not afraid of the younger guys. She will cuss one of them out in a minute and they will think it is so adorable because she reminds them of their mothers. Plus, they can get special privileges from the cougar like staying up late and extended telephone and TV use. If you are older then you need to be mindful of how you treat her because many inmates in the younger crowd look at the cougar as a mother figure. If you get into an argument with her please apologize to her openly. You don't need fifteen twenty-year-old prisoners punching you in the face at one time. Trust me, that hurts. Swallow your pride, not your teeth. This lady is not wrong for not wanting to be bothered with you. The truth is that the judge and people of the court didn't want to be bothered by you either.

Use this prison time to give yourself some attention. Study law books, history, and math. Your brain is a tool that needs to be sharpened just like a pencil. One of the worst things that you can do is get into a confrontation with a female officer because you will end up looking foolish most of the time and people won't respect you.

Next you have the troublemaker. This female officer is and can be very dangerous. She abuses her power by promoting hate and jealousy amongst the prison population. She will tell one inmate that another inmate snitched on him for one reason or another. The inmate will assault the inmate whom he believes snitched on him. Both inmates will get put in segregation and the lady troublemaker will be laughing about the whole ordeal with her coworkers because she made the snitching story up. Nine times out of ten her informant (the person you see talking to her regularly) is the one who did the snitching. She just picked that particular inmate to lie on because maybe she didn't like his hair or he thought he was tough. Her objective is to be entertained by any means necessary. If this means someone might get his/her head busted open then so be it. Most of these female troublemakers are between twenty-three and thirty-five years old.

She is usually very loud and flashy. The troublemaker is also a pathological liar. She will lie about any and everything. Her biggest lie is the amount of money she has in the bank. She will exaggerate her net worth dramatically. Most inmates will believe her because she might drive a new car or sport an expensive watch. The troublemaker will convince others that she really doesn't need her job and her family is very wealthy.

She will tell you that her brothers are notorious drug dealers. All she has to do is make a phone call and she can get anybody taken out. Her entire life is a complex maze of fabrications. The truth is that she squanders her money on frivolous things like fake hair, expensive clothes, fast food, and alcohol. She can't keep a decent man in her life so she settles for abusive relationships. This lady will allow her boyfriend to beat up on her as long as he looks like Chris Brown or some R&B star. The troublemaker is usually the product of a dysfunctional family (crackhead parents). She may have grown up in foster homes or group homes. If you ignore her she will take that as a sign of disrespect. She will grow to hate you and her ego will tell her that she needs to assassinate your character. If she can't get any negative information on you then she will make something up.

The best way to avoid her havoc is by simply speaking to her every now and then. Your acknowledgement of her presence will pacify her ego. You may have to listen to one of her great adventures that she had with her drug dealing brother or boyfriend. You don't have to listen to her rambling on and on. Excuse yourself and tell her you have to use the restroom. I'm not telling you to be superficial, but being somewhat cordial with the female troublemaker might be a wise decision because she can be a problem if she does not feel wanted due to her troubled past. In most cases the people that she works for (Sgt., Lt., Cpt.) are the only real family the troublemaker has. They feel sorry for her because her life outside of work is pathetic. She even uses them to co-sign loans for cars and homes because nobody outside of those prison walls really cares about her.

One thing that I have learned about women is that they see and hear better than most men. It's almost like they have eyes in the back of their heads. Be very careful of what you say and do because you might think the female officer can't hear your conversation, but she is listening and taking mental notes on your mannerisms.

These women have excellent peripheral vision. You might think she is reading the newspaper but her eyes are on you the whole time. I believe that women have a greater flow of extra sensory perception (ESP) than men. That's why women are very sensitive most of the time. Don't be alarmed if the female officer speaks to you on Monday and ignores you on Tuesday because women have very strange temperaments. She can feel happy one minute and sad the next. Women have a natural right to be this way due to the tribulations they face in life such as childbearing, menstruation, menopause, etc. Most women expect the men to be able to deal with their temperaments and still remain the solid rocks that we are or should be. Guess what? She is very right to expect this from a man. You should never treat a woman in a manner that you wouldn't want your mother, sister, or wife to be treated in. I wouldn't advise you to look down on these women because they work in a prison. These women have responsibilities along with bills to pay. You can't knock her hustle. Let that woman live her life without feeling your misery and pain. It's not her fault you chose a life of crime. Smile when you see her because she is a gift and a blessing. Try to offer words of inspiration to these ladies. You don't have to give a sermon of Kuthbar but we all can use a few words of encouragement every now and then.

You have to remember that many of those female officers also have husbands, sons, grandsons, and nephews behind those prison walls. They understand exactly what you are going through, so stop going at them like they can't feel your pain because you are no different from her knuckleheaded son or daughter. You have to ask yourself how you would feel if your wife, mother, or sister worked as a female correctional officer and people were using profanity in place of her name and exposing their private parts in front of her, being nasty and disrespectful. I know you think that no female in your family would ever take a job in a prison but in these hard times a job is a job. Respect these women and show them you have self control. A few of them may act rude toward you but you have to understand the stress they are under. You have some inmates and officers who stalk these ladies all day. These women are being sexually harassed and constantly being put down by miserable inmates. They have to deal with murderers, child molesters, and rapists. Some of these women are physically and sexually assaulted at some point in their careers.

Karma is very real so treat people like you want to be treated. I'm not saying you have to worship the ground the female officer walks on, but you could show a little understanding concerning her. I wouldn't recommend you becoming romantically involved with a female correctional officer because this involvement with her may backfire in the long run. Most female correctional officers have a number of inmates that they wish to be romantically linked with. You would be crazy to think that you are the only one. If you don't have a problem with that then it's cool. I personally think that a person who brings romance into an environment like prison is somewhat crazy. Prison is a haven for diseases like MRSA, hepatitis, tuberculosis and AIDS.

Truthfully speaking a number of these female officers have low self esteem and tend to practice poor judgment. All I'm saying is that you are taking a big risk by being romantically involved with a person who practices poor judgment. You could come in contact with one of the diseases listed above. The only point that I'm trying to make is that your health and well being should never ride on any risky behavior that can cause sickness.

Your objective should be geared towards educating yourself so that these prison doors don't become revolving doors. You have to rehabilitate yourself. In other words you should be concentrating on you and not that lady in the blue uniform. I know it's not easy but stay in the books and your reward will be very beneficial to you.

5

Thou Shalt Maintain Physical Fitness

This chapter would probably be my most favorite subject. Physical fitness can lead you mental and spiritual fitness. Most of the people who I have been in prison with would probably describe me as a beast when it comes to working out and lifting weights. There have been times when I would work out for four and five hours a day, seven days a week.

I went from being lazy at the beginning of my prison sentence to having an impeccable work ethic at the end. If you have any kind of sickness or disease it would be wise to check with the doctor for permission to lift weights and exercise. There is a lot of politics involved with working out in prison. Everyone behind bars is a fitness expert of some sort. When you start working out on the yard people will tell you that you are working out the wrong way and proceed to tell you the correct way. This will become quite confusing and annoying after your third or fourth session.

You have to remember that prison is full of con artists and liars. Some of these guys are waiting to catch you at the weight pile because they know that you are probably lazy and looking for a workout partner. Once you start to bench press those two forty-five pound plates your new workout partner will virtually appear out of nowhere ready to spot and assist you through your next few sets. There is a thirty percent chance of his/her intentions being honorable, and a seventy percent chance that he/she is trying to befriend you for food, money, and/or sex.

Don't panic if this happens to you because in prison you are not judged by what happens to you, but you are judged by how you handle what happens to you. When you show emotions you appear to be weak. I can help you avoid the above situation by doing a few things. The first thing you need to do is let that person know in a cool and polite manner that you would prefer to work out alone. If he/she persists on helping you then walk away and work out at another time. The second thing you need to do is take a good look at everyone around you. Find the person who is serious about lifting weights and if his/her physique is the kind of body that wouldn't mind looking like, then that person should be your workout partner/coach.

Be thoughtful of how you approach this person. Let him/her see you working out alone for two or three months. You can find workout routines in magazines like Men's Health or Muscle and Fitness. Don't become confused by all of the different workout routines that you will come across in these magazines. These different routines are not designed to confuse you but they are designed to confuse your muscles. Fitness experts have learned that when you repeat the same workout routine over and over again your muscles will get familiar with it and stop growing. This is why you have to constantly switch from one type of workout to another so that you may be able to confuse your muscles. Confused muscles have a tendency to grow.

The people who create those health and fitness magazines understand that your muscles need confusion so they present us with new workout routines every month. Almost every inmate will at some point use one or both of these fitness magazines as a guide. The reason that you should want to find a workout partner/coach is all in your form. You can follow the instructions in your workout plan all day, but if you're not using the proper physical form when exercising you won't see any major results and you are also risking an injury.

Your workout partner can show you the proper form and motivate you at the same time. Never approach a potential workout partner/coach while they are in the middle of his/her routine. Most people who are dedicated to physical fitness don't like to lose focus during a workout session. This means that he/she may give you the silent treatment if you approach them while they are exercising. It would be feasible for you to wait until you see him/her in the dining hall or day room. Don't beat around the bush when you start to converse. Let him/her know that you noticed how dedicated they are to physical fitness and if it's not too much trouble would he/she provide you with a few workout tips.

Unless he/she has some type of bipolar disorder the answer should be yes. Most people who exercise on a regular basis love to help others do the same. Don't forget to watch this guy for at least thirty days before you approach him/her. Make sure he/she isn't into anything crazy because judge you by the company you keep. Your workout partner/coach will most likely have been incarcerated for a while and is very motivated during his/her training sessions. This means that he/she may be very strict on you when you begin to work with him/her. Don't be surprised if your trainer yells at you or gets frustrated because most of the people in prison are not certified with the National Academy of Sports and Medicine. It's okay if you are yelled at every now and then. Think of yourself as a Marine in basic training. You can't allow your trainer to try these tactics when the both of you are not working out. There is no need for your trainer to raise his/her voice at you outside of the weight pile. If he/she does this it's your duty to calmly let him/her know that it's okay for him/her to treat you in that manner during your training session but that's as far as it will go. If this happens to you don't take it personally. Most of the inmates who are into health and fitness have been in prison for years and they are perfectionists. He/she really doesn't mean you any harm if they attempt to correct you when the both of you are not working out. He/she is more than likely concerned with your overall well being. You will have to stand your ground and be firm with your trainer/coach.

You might not want a workout partner for many reasons. That's cool but you need to be sure that you are exercising properly. If you are overweight with that spare tire hanging around your waist it would be wise for you to lose weight before you start lifting heavy weights. I can't count how many times I have seen that overweight guy bench pressing three hundred and twenty five pounds until he gets tired, and after he leaves the weight pile he will eat four chicken sandwiches, six fudge rounds, and drink three sodas. After he finishes his last soda he will belch real loud and then look at me and say, "Man I wish I looked like you." This guy is living in a fantasy world. He may even believe that because his arms feel tight that he is in good shape. This would explain why you see that fat guy with his short sleeves rolled up all the time.

If this is you please don't feel embarrassed because you should give yourself an A for your effort. Your biggest problem is that you have placed yourself on a reward system. A reward system is what happens after you finish working out. You say to yourself, "I worked really hard so now I deserve to eat a big meal." You keep gaining weight but you somehow convince yourself that it's muscle. Stop that! Start drinking water after you work out. Don't eat anything after eight o'clock p.m. You can lift weights but that's only the first half of your workout. The second half of your workout is strictly cardiovascular.

Cardiovascular is relating to or involving the heart and the blood vessels. Your other half of the workout is designed to strengthen your heart so that blood and oxygen can flow easily to your muscles. When blood and oxygen can flow easily through your body, your muscles will respond by growing. But in order to get your blood flowing means that you have to burn fat. I have witnessed skinny people build amazing muscle mass because they had no fat to burn off so the blood and oxygen went straight to their muscles. You can achieve these results by running, walking, push-ups, sit-ups, pull-ups, and shadow boxing. Some prison facilities might not allow running in the yard but you can do jumping jacks instead.

Your workout sessions should be no less than one hour every day. If you have high blood pressure, don't forget to check with the doctor or nurse at your facility before working out. I don't expect you to work out seven days out of every week in your beginning stages. I do expect you to strive for five days a week. Okay, here is the good part. I want you to pick a cheat day. A cheat day is when you reward yourself for staying with your workout plan. You eat whatever you want, whenever you want. I would advise you to pick this day between Friday and Sunday and dedicate yourself on the other days. When you pig out on your cheat day please remember to elevate your head over your shoulders before you rest at night. You can do this by simply propping your pillow in the correct position under your head. This will allow your body to properly digest your food when you sleep.

Your goal is to sweat and sweat some more. That's your body telling you that you are doing a good job. If you are not sweating while exercising then you are playing around. Don't be afraid to burn that fat off. I know jumping around and doing push-ups might make you feel a little humiliated around people, but don't you already feel a little humiliated about being out of shape? You might feel awkward at first but in time you will pat yourself on the back for exercising. Your energy level will shoot through the roof. Everything speeds up after that. Your brain works faster and you feel light on your feet. You will have a better outlook on life in general and your conversations with other people will be more positive. You will also take notice on how slowly people are moving that are around you. Don't laugh when you see that guy who comes to the weight pile and does a set of curls and then he will just sit there staring into space for the next ten minutes. You used to do the same thing.

If you smoke cigarettes don't expect to see any major results. Cigarette smoke blocks oxygen from flowing to your muscles and lungs. That's why people who lift weights and smoke cigarettes hardly ever see any muscle growth. Most people who smoke appear to have big arms and a small chest or a big chest and small arms. Cigarette smoke alters and distorts your muscle growth.

Don't forget to keep changing your workout routine. You can lift weights during the first half of your session and do cardio the second half, or cardio the first half and lift weights the second. The key is confusing your muscles. Confused muscles grow faster. Your body is a lot smarter than you think. I used to think of what body part that I was going to work on the night before my workout, and I would literally feel the body parts that I wanted to work on tensing up all through the night. My muscles had read my brain pattern and they decided to get prepared for the workout the next day.

Once I caught on to what my muscles were doing I had to start confusing them by changing my routine on a weekly basis. One week would look like this:

Monday-	squats, pull-ups, sit-ups
Tuesday-	chest, push-ups, jog
Wednesday-	arms, jumping jacks, sit-ups
Thursday-	back, play basketball, pull-ups, dips
Friday-	shoulders, jog, pull-ups, sit-ups
Saturday-	pull-ups, dips, push-ups, sit-ups
Sunday-	jog, squats, play basketball, sit-ups

The next week would look like this:

Monday-	back, play basketball, pull-ups, dips
Tuesday-	shoulders, jog, pull-ups, sit-ups
Wednesday-	pull-ups, dips, push-ups, sit-ups
Thursday-	jog, squats, play basketball, sit-ups
Friday-	squats, pull-ups, sit-ups
Saturday-	chest, push-ups, jog
Sunday-	arms, jumping jacks, sit-ups

If you noticed I have sit-ups listed for many days during the week. You will need different types of sit-ups when you work out such as crunches, bicycles, and leg raises. Look in the Muscle and Fitness magazine to learn different routines.

Now you don't have to take advice from the guy in the weight pile eating a honey bun and using the weight bench for a recliner.

6

THOU SHALT MAINTAIN A HEALTHY DIET WITH GOOD NUTRITION

Unfortunately you don't have much of a selection of food and drinks in prison. I would advise anyone who is suffering from any type of sickness or disease to talk with the doctor about receiving a special diet. The truth is that the less you eat the longer you live. It's not healthy to eat until your stomach feels full. This will only put a strain on your digestive tract. Access to food that your body does not digest can destroy your intestines, stick to your colon, and clog your arteries. All of these things can lead to chronic illnesses such as heart disease and cancer.

Nutritionists have recently stated that it is healthy to fast for at least one day out of every week. When you stop eating for a short period of time your body shuts down and begins to get rid of harmful toxins. Once this happens you begin to feel lighter and your organs start functioning better than before. If your stomach is full and you need to lie down after every meal you are overeating. Stop this immediately.

The problem that most overeaters have is that when they pig out the brain can't detect when he/she is overeating. That means the brain doesn't send signals to stop us from consuming too much food.

If you over indulge then you are killing yourself. Maybe you are depressed and food is the only thing that makes you feel better. (Refer to Chapter 1 for depression.) Depression is a mental disorder and if you feel out of control please seek professional help.

Meat is a source of protein but if you consume too much you are setting yourself up for failure. I am a vegan and my diet excludes meat, eggs, milk, and butter. People always ask me why I decided to go on a vegan diet. No matter what kind of meat I would eat my stomach would get upset. I thought maybe something was wrong with my digestive system, so I made an appointment with the doctor. He said I was ok and gave me a box of Metamucil.

The Metamucil helped a little because it's fiber taken from plants, but I would still have stomach pains after every meal. I began to read a newspaper that someone had left on a table in front of me. The newspaper stated that the government was testing the human consumption of closed cows and chickens inside of the prison population. Evidently the FDA was satisfied with the results of this test because they began placing cloned meats on the shelves of grocery stores all over the U.S. in 2006.

I stopped eating meat that same day and I have never felt better in my life. My only problem was that I needed a source of protein. Fortunately there was a nutritionist working at the prison. She informed me that beans are a great source of protein. Beans also contain a chemical called lycopene. Lyconpene is a natural element that fights cancer.

I started substituting meat with beans and rice. The combination was ok but my stomach would still be a little upset after I ate. After weeks of complaining about the beans and rice to my workout partner, he showed me another article in the newspaper.

This article stated that a group of college kids had invented synthetic rice and had received permission from the government to grow over eighty acres of the fake rice in North Carolina, the same state I was incarcerated in. This rice is supposed to be better for humans and is said to help fight the common cold, according to the newspaper. Well, you definitely guessed correctly if you guessed that I stopped eating rice. That's right, no meat, rice, milk, eggs, or butter and I feel great.

I will admit that bench pressing two hundred and thirty-five pounds seems heavier but I have more speed and stamina now. Most prisons will allow anyone to go on a vegan diet but it will have to be for religious purposes. You will need to talk to the Chaplain at your facility. Make sure your money is sufficient if you decide to go on a vegan diet. Unless you enjoy beans and cabbage every day, I would advise you to snack on peanuts and cookies from the canteen every now and then.

Don't abuse this advice and start eating too many sweets. Sugar destroys your DNA. Sugar turns into fat when your body stops burning calories. You can work out all day long, but you will not see any results if your calorie intake is too high.

The average person should not consume more that thirty-five hundred calories per day. This might sound easy but one cupcake can have as many a three hundred calories. The bottom line is that if you want to look great you have to burn calories. You can run, walk, do sit-ups or whatever gets you motivated, but if you eat and sleep all day it will show.

I can't stress enough the importance of exercising to burn fat. There have been times when I would work out and finally get a firm stomach or six-pack, as some may call it. I might reward myself with a pint of butter pecan ice cream. As soon as I ate the ice cream my six-pack would turn into a four-pack. That's how serious burning fat can be.

Some fat is called good because it burns into fuel for your muscles when you exercise. That fat is called Omega-three fat. You can find Omega-three fatty acids in items like fish and vegetable oil. Other fatty acids are called Omega-six and they can be found in meats like pork and beef. Omega-six fatty acids are the hardest to burn.

If this sounds complicated and stressful to you maybe you should talk about your diet with your workout partner. You may decide to go on a diet but kick yourself in the rear end if you cheat a few times. Scientists have proven that if you slip up and cheat on you diet the stress that you might feel from messing up can cause you to gain weight. Remember, if you slip up on your diet don't worry about it. You will have to work harder during your next workout routine. Worrying about your diet will harm you in the long run.

Don't be fooled by soft drinks that are disguised as fruit juice or bottled water. These drinks are our enemies. They are packaged to make us believe we will benefit from drinking them. All you have to do is read the ingredients and look for words like 'high fructose', 'corn syrup', and 'Yellow #5.' When you see these ingredients get away from that bottle immediately. These ingredients are sugars and if you drink just one soft drink a day you can gain as much as five pounds a week.

I can't tell you enough about the benefits of fruits and vegetables. When eating red fruits and vegetables, including tomatoes, berries, peppers, and radishes, you take in nutrients such as lycopene, ellagic acid, quercetin, and hesperidin to name a few.

These nutrients reduce the risk of prostate cancer, lower blood pressure, reduce tumor growth and LDL cholesterol levels, scavenge harmful free radicals, and support joint tissue in arthritis cases.

Carrots, yams, squash, papayas, and other orange and yellow fruits and vegetables contain betacarotene, zeaxanthin, flavonoids, lycopene, potassioum, and vitamin C. These nutrients reduce age related macular degeneration and the risk of prostate cancer, lower LDL cholesterol and blood pressure, promote collagen formation and healthy joints, fight harmful free radicals, encourage alkaline balance, and work with magnesium and calcium to build healthy bones.

White fruits and vegetables, including mushrooms, white tea, flaxseed and pumpkin, contain nutrients such as betaglucans, EGCG and lignans that provide powerful immune system boosting activity.

These nutrients also activate natural virus killer B and T-cells, reduce the risk of colon, breast and prostate cancers, and balance hormone levels, reducing the risk of hormone related cancers. Wheatgrass, barley grass, oat grass, kale, spinach, cabbage, alfalfa sprouts, mustard greens, and collard greens are all examples of green vegetables that contain chlorophyll, fiber, lutien, zeaxanthin, calcium folate, vitamin C, calcium and beta carotene. The nutrients found in these vegetables reduce cancer risks, lower blood pressure and LDL cholesterol levels, normalize digestion time, support retinal health and vision, fight harmful free radicals, and boost immune system activity.

Blue and purple fruits and vegetables such as blueberries, pomegranates, grapes, elderberries, eggplant, and prunes contain nutrients which include lutein, zeaxanthin, resveratrol, vitamin C, fiber, flavonoids, ellagic acid, and quercetin. Similar to the previous nutrients, these nutrients support retinal health, lower LDL cholesterol, boost immune system activity, support healthy digestion, improve calcium and other mineral absorption, fight inflammation, reduce tumor growth, act as an anti-carcinogen in the digestive tract, and limit the activity of cancer cells.

These nutrients that are found in the above listed fruits and vegetables can have a significant impact on our health. Quercitin, which is found in apples, onions, and other citrus fruits, not only prevents LDL cholesterol oxidation, but also helps the body cope with allergens and other lung and breathing problems. Ellagic acid, which is mainly found in raspberries, strawberries, pomegranates and walnuts, has been proven in many clinical studies to act as an antioxidant and anti-carcinogen in the gastrointestinal tract. This nutrient also has been proven to have an anti-proliferative effect on cancer cells, because it decreases their ATP production.

The best known of the carotenoids, beta carotene, is converted into Vitamin A upon entering the liver. Although it's known for its positive effects on eyesight it also has been proven to decrease cholesterol levels in the liver. Clinical studies have proven lycopene, mainly found in tomatoes, may reduce the risk of prostate cancer as well as protect against heart disease. Lutein, which is found in blueberries and members of the squash family, is important for healthy eyes. However it does support your heart too, helping to protect against coronary heart disease.

Along with the above nutrients there are even more nutrients found in fruits and vegetables that provide a great deal of support to the body.

Almost everyone has heard of Vitamin C, which keeps our immune system strong, speeds wound healing, and promotes strong muscles and joints. This nutrient is scattered throughout the spectrum of fruits, but is commonly associated with oranges and other citrus fruits. Potassium, which is the nutrient most Americans are deficient in, does great things for out hearts and lowers blood pressure.

Another good food component many people don't get enough of is fiber, found in fruits, vegetables, and whole grains. Flavanoids, which include anthocyanins, flavones, isoflavones, quercetin and more, are found almost everywhere. They are responsible for the color of skins in fruits and vegetables and help stop the growth of tumor cells and are potent antioxidants. They also can reduce inflammation. Beta-glucan, found in mushrooms, stabilizes and balances the body's immune system by supporting white blood cells.

EGCG is found in tea and has been shown to reduce the risk of colon and breast cancer. It boosts the immune system and encourages t-cell formation, which defends our body against sickness and disease. Lastly, bioflavanoids, which are found in citrus fruits, are considered companions of vitamin C because they extend their value in the body. These nutrients have the capabilities to lower cholesterol levels and support joint collagen in arthritis cases.

The number one excuse for not eating the required

five servings of fruits and vegetables each day is that they are too expensive. However compared to the amount of prepackaged, processed, and fast foods, most fruits and vegetables are not that expensive.

Because frozen fruits and vegetables retain the majority of their nutritional value they can be an excellent alternative when certain foods are out of season. Someone who is not able to eat five servings of fruits and vegetable each day can also drink fruit and vegetable drinks in their place, although this shouldn't become a habit.

The need for fruits and vegetables is growing rapidly with cases of type-2 diabetes, heart disease, high cholesterol, and hypertension that result from the typical American diet of fatty meats, processed sugars and refined grains.

The information in this chapter can be found online under 'The Colors of Health' and 'The Color Wheel of Fruits and Vegetables.'

Think smart and eat smart. You will feel much better and live a healthier life. Remember, you shouldn't eat after 8 PM to allow you digestive tract to wok properly. Drink plenty of water. Bottled water is the better choice between tap and bottled water because there are times when the government will advise the public to boil tap water before drinking it. If you were to put a sample of tap water under a microscope you would probably think you were at a circus. Plus tap water can carry high levels of mercury that can put black and purple blotches on your skin. Staying healthy is the key to a good life. It's your life and you only live once.

7

Thou Shalt Put God First
(Religion and Spirituality)

Some people frown at the word religion. They think the concept of religion is old and outdated. This is very far from the truth. Studies have shown that people who follow a certain type of religion generally live better and more productive lives than those who don't follow religion. The Bible's laws are the basic fundamentals used in Narcotics Anonymous and Alcoholics Anonymous. These two groups hold record numbers of people who live productive lives after following a twelve step program.

You can definitely benefit tremendously in believing a higher power exists and by following a religion. Most religions teach good moral and ethical values. These values usually range in a variety of topics such as social development, childrearing, and keeping your body clean and disease free. I know you've heard the old saying that 'cleanliness is next to godliness.' The truth is that most of us who have moved away from religion have shamed ourselves in some form or another. We have become dirty, so to speak. With that in mind let's look at the meaning of the word religion. The prefix 're-' means to go back or do again. The 'ligion' in the word religion comes from the Greek word 'lagion,' which means to tie down or bind. Therefore the word religion means to go back and tie or bind yourself back to the Creator. If cleanliness is next to godliness then religion is the way to clean our lives up.

In prison there are a few religions that are available for you to learn. I am about to go into detail, but before I go any further you need to understand that whatever religion you decide to join or have already joined, there are good and evil people who participate in every religion known to mankind. People are people and we all make mistakes, so if you see your pastor, Imam, Grand Sheik or one of your peers do something that goes against your teachings don't use that as an excuse to stop studying and obeying God's word because it is natural for human beings to make errors. If you don't believe me just take a look at some of the mistakes you have made.

Don't allow someone's poor judgment to stop the blessings that God desires to place in your life. Some religions teach us that anyone who is a new member of a particular faith is actually the purest or most righteous of the group. The new member is considered precious like a new born baby and is expected to set an example of purity to the older members.

Your main objective is the seek God first. This means you have to learn what His will is and how his laws or commandments can benefit your life. This can only be done through studying the word of God.

People often ask me questions like, 'What religion should I join?' or, 'How do I know if it's the right one?'

Join whatever religion makes the most sense to you. There may come a point in time when the faith you are with becomes questionable and you may find another religion that makes more sense of life. If that other religion seems better for you then join it.

You have to remember that as you study God's word you become wiser and things become clearer, so if you have a different insight on life than you did six months earlier, and this new religion seems to compliment your view about what the Creator's will in your life ought to be then go ahead and seek the kingdom of God first and join that new faith. Who knows, you might decide to join a third group or religion after that.

This might go against what you were taught or what you are learning but the truth is that the more you study the wiser you become. Trust me, God does not frown upon wisdom. You won't be committing a sin. People die because of ignorance. King Solomon was considered a very wise man and he wrote a couple books in the Bible (Proverbs and The Song of Solomon). The wise men who brought Jesus gifts were considered righteous.

Some people study religion to match wits or debate with other religious leaders. Don't fall into that trap. Religion was not created for that purpose. People who do that have missed out on God's blessings because they use his word as a tool to destroy their fellow man. If you do this stop! If you know somebody who does this stay away from them, because if you are new-born in your faith they will try to crush your sincere intentions to serve the Creator. Don't worry about them because they with have to answer to God on the day of judgment. Be aware of those prisoners who use religion as a means to take advantage of kindhearted people. These prisoners join certain faiths just to get food, cigarettes, toothpaste, and soap from those good religious prisoners. There is nothing wrong with giving but you can't allow someone to mistake your kindness for weakness. When you follow God's commandments then all of life's situations will become clear to you with the wisdom to deal with these situations in accordance to God's law.

I hope I cleared some things up for you. Now I am about to explain some of the religions that you may join in prison.

Christianity- The history of Christianity is really the history of Western civilization. Christianity has had an all pervasive influence on society at large. Art, language, politics, law, family life, calendar dates, music, and the very way we think have all been colored by Christian influence for almost tow millennia. The story of the Church, therefore, is an important one to know.

The Church began 40 days after Jesus' resurrection (c. A.D. 35). Jesus had promised that he would build his Church (Matthew 16:18), and with the coming of the Holy Spirit on the day of Pentecost (Acts 2: 1-4) the Church (the called-out assembly) officially began. Three thousand people responded to Peter's sermon that day and chose to follow Christ.

The initial converts to Christianity were Jews of proselytes to Judaism and the Church was centered in Jerusalem. Because of this, Christianity was at first seen as a Jewish sect, akin to the Pharisees, Saducees, of the Essenes. However, what the apostles preached was radically different from what other Jewish groups were teaching. Jesus was the Jewish Messiah (the anointed king) who had come to fulfill the Law (Matthew 5:17) and institute a New Covenant based on His death (Mark 14:24). This message, with its charge that they had killed their own Messiah, infuriated many Jewish leaders, and some, like Saul of Tarsus, took action to stamp out 'The Way" (Acts 9: 1-2).

It's quite proper to say that Christianity has its roots in Judaism. The Old Testament laid the groundwork for the New, and it is impossible to fully understand Christianity without a working knowledge of the Old Testament (See the books of Matthew and Hebrews). The Old Testament explains the necessity of a Messiah, contains the history of the Messiah's people, and predicts the Messiah's coming. The New Testament then is all about the coming of the Messiah and His work to save us form sin. In His life Jesus fulfilled over 300 specific prophecies, proving that He was the One the Old Testament had anticipated.

Not long after Pentecost the doors to the Church were opened to non-Jews. The Evangelist Philip preached to the Samaritans (Acts 8:5), and many of them believed in Christ. The Apostle Peter preached to the Gentile household of Cornelius (Acts 10) and they too received the Holy Spirit. The Apostle Paul (the former persecutor of the Church) spread the gospel (good news) all over the Greco-Roman world, reaching as far as Rome itself (Acts 28:16) and possibly all the way to Spain.

By A.D. 70, the year Jerusalem was destroyed, the books of the New Testament had mostly been completed and were circulating among the churches. For the next 240 years Christians were persecuted by Rome, sometimes at random, sometimes by government edict.

In the second and third centuries, the church leadership

became more and more hierarchal as numbers increased. Several heresies were exposed and refuted during this time, and the New Testament canon was agreed upon. Persecution continued to intensify. (You can find this on www.gotquestions.org).

Then in A.D. 312 the Roman Emperor Constantine claimed to have a conversion experience. About 70 years later, during the reign of Theodosius, Christianity became the official religion of the Roman Empire. Bishops were given places of honor in the government, and by A.D. 400 the terms Roman and Christian were virtually synonymous.

After Constantine the Christians were no longer persecuted. In time it was the pagans who came under persecution unless they 'converted' to Christianity. Such forced conversions led to many people entering the church without a true change of heart. The pagans brought with them their idols and the practices they were accustomed to, and the Church's changed icons, elaborate architecture, pilgrimages, and the veneration of saints were added to the simplicity of early church worship. About this same time some Christians retreated from Rome, choosing to live in isolation as monks, and infant baptism was introduced as a means of washing away original sin.

Throughout the next few centuries various church councils were held in an attempt to determine the Church's official doctrine, to censure clerical abuses, and to make peace between warring factions. As the Roman Empire grew weaker the Church became more powerful, and many disagreements broke out between the churches in the West and those in the East. The Western (Latin) Church, based in Rome, claimed apostolic authority over all churches. The Bishop of Rome had begun calling himself the 'Pope' (the Father). This did not sit well with the Eastern (Greek) Church based in Constantinople. Theological, political, procedural, and linguistic divides all contributed to the Great Schism in 1054 in with the Roman Catholic (Universal) Church and the Eastern Orthodox excommunicated each other and broke all ties.

During the Middle Ages in Europe the Roman Catholic Church continued to hold power, with the Pope's claiming authority over all levels of life and living as kings. Corruption and greed in the church leadership was commonplace. From 1095 to 1204 A.D. the popes endorsed a serried of bloody and expensive crusades in an effort to repel Muslim advances and liberate Jerusalem.

Through the years several individuals had tried to call attention to the theological, political, and human rights abuses of the Roman Church. All had been silenced in one way or another. But in 1517 a German monk named Martin Luther took a stand against the Church and everyone heard. With Luther came the Protestant Reformation and the Middle Ages came to a close.

The Reformers, including Luther, Calvin, and Zwingli, differed on many finer points of theology, but they were consistent in their emphasis on the Bible's supreme authority over church tradition and the fact that sinners are saved by grace through faith alone apart from works (Ephesians 2: 8-9).

The New Testament taught that Jesus the Messiah should be worshipped and trusted, which is to say He is co-equally God and man. The New Testament forbids the worship of angels (Colossians 2: 18, Revelation 22: 8-9) but commands worship of Jesus. The Apostle Paul tells us that, "in Christ all the fullness of Deity lives in bodily form" (Colossians 2:9, 1:19). Paul declares Jesus as Lord and the One to whom a person must pray for salvation just as one calls on Jehovah Yahweh (Joel 2:32, Romans 10: 9-13). "Jesus is God overall," (Romans 9:5) and our God and Savior (Titus 2:13). Faith in Jesus' deity is basic to Paul's testimony and theology.

John's gospel declares Jesus to be the Divine Eternal Logos, agent of creation and source of life and light (John 1: 1-5,9), "the Way, the Truth, and the Life" (John 14:6), an advocate with the Heavenly Father (I John 2: 1-2), sovereign (Revelation 1:5), the rider on a white horse (Revelation 19: 11-16), and the totality of the son of God from the beginning to the end (Revelation 22: 13). This information was provided by Got Questions Ministries (www.gotquestions.org/printer/council-nicea-pf.html).

Islam- When Muhammad (pbuh) reached the mature age of forty years his wisdom and strength of character were well known to everybody in Mecca. This was especially of his wife, Khadija the Pure.

The previous months that year had seen Muhammad to be increasingly contemplating at Hiraa Cave. His aim, as always, was the constant search for Truth. It was a very difficult period to go through. Even Muhammad himself had feelings of uneasiness about what he was going through. On several occasions he discussed his fears with his wife, Khadija, looking for assurance and support.

Instead of becoming worried or disturbed about him, Khadija comforted, assured, and supported him. She gave him the very things he needed, sincerely from the bottom of her heart.

It was the month of Ramadhan, and once again

Muhammad went into seclusion in the cave Hiraa. He kept searching his mind as he had done before so many times.

One day Muhammad was asleep in the cave and it was very quiet there. Muhammad was awakened by some being. "READ!" Muhammad heard the word and the whole cave echoed with it! Muhammad got scared and his heart beat very fast. Muhammad had never learned how to read or write. He was what is called unlettered. So he answered, "But I cannot read." He did not know to whom he was answering. Muhammad felt as if something was gripping him and squeezing him hard.

He was relieved for a short while just to hear again the commanding voice say, "READ!" Upon hearing that Muhammad answered again, "But I cannot read." Once again he felt as if he was being squeezed hard and then released.

Then for a third time the voice commanded "READ!" This time Muhammad said, "What shall I read?" and he heard:

"Read in the name of your Lord who creates:
He created man from a cell.

Read and your Lord is most generous,
Who taught by the pen,

He taught man what he knew not."

Muhammad repeated those words and he felt as if they were engraved in his mind. He could never shake those words out of his mind. They were there, fixed right in his mind. Muhammad became more curious than ever, especially when he couldn't see the source of the voice. He waited in the Hiraa Cave for a short while scared stiff and then he ran out of it. He wanted to escape, to get out fast, very fast. It took him about half an hour to come down the Mountain of Noor.

When he was at the bottom of the mountain to his surprise he heard someone calling, "Muhammad, Muhammad!" Muhammad looked up and saw the image of a man shining brightly with light. The shining man had wings that filled the space between the skies and the earth. The shining man with wings moved in every direction Mohammed moved. It made Muhammad feel sure it was not an illusion, that he was seeing something real.

"I am Gabriel, Muhammad. I am Allah's messenger to His prophets. You are His prophet and you will guide humanity to the right path, the path of truth."

Thus, with such strange and beautiful words, the angel Gabriel announced the prophethood of Muhammad (pbuh). Once said in a commanding way, that figure of a man disappeared. The angel was gone. Muhammad was left alone feeling weak, pale, and tired. He was feeling sick. His head was swimming with notions and ideas. He was almost disoriented.

Having now become Allah's messenger, Muhammad (pbuh) took on the heavy responsibility of calling to the people of Islam. Though his first few converts were his family, then closest friends, slowly and gradually Islam began to gain new converts from the very poor, meek and some of the slaves. Though most of the new Muslims were the insignificant and weak who were not influential, their new faith changed them into strong, dynamic persons of iron will. These new Muslims constituted the backbone of the early Islamic Ummah (Islamic Community).

The new Muslims frequently visited Muhammad to receive lessons in Islam, to learn more about it, and to learn all about what was revealed of the Holy Quran up to the time.

A number of people in Mecca started to hear about Muhammad (pbuh), the new religion called Islam, and the new group of converts. Some thought Muhammad was insane, others thought he was a magician, while others thought he was after fame or some material gain. They laughed in sarcasm when they considered the new Muslims since they were the weak, insignificant, slaves or the like. As a matter of fact the Meccans believed their idols would shield them against Muhammad (pbuh) and Islam!

The word of Islam began to spread however, since the Message was calling to the belief in the Truth. It was noble that it called for decency, truthfulness, and sincerity in the service of Allah, the Creator. The call was for justice in the society in all dealings, for a decent living, and a life of dynamic conscience directly responsible to Allah (swt).

The Meccans underestimated the powerful Islamic Message, or the power of faith. Three long years passed and the message of Islam was still being spread in secret, and Muhammad the Prophet had a growing but limited number of followers. As more and more people heard about Islam and the Message spread more widely, a command from the Almighty was revealed to Mohammed (pbuh) to call people to Islam in a public manner.

The message of Islam was not to be propagated anymore in secret. This bold step was to be taken immediately and higher risks were thus in store. It was a giant step forward and Islam's followers were ready for the tough days ahead, and for the encounter with the disbelievers who were the overwhelming majority. The stage was set for the Prophet (pbuh) and the small Muslim Ummah on the one hand versus the disbelievers in the other hand. The information you read was provided by *Life of Muhammad* (pbuh) Volume 1, prepared by A.S. Hashim, M.D.

Moorish Science Temple of America- Noble Drew Ali is the founder of the Moorish Science Temple of America. He founded the temple in 1913 A.D. The Moorish Science Temple was founded in Newark, New Jersey. Noble Drew Ali was born in the state of North Carolina in 1886. Noble Drew Ali's nationality is Moorish-American. Moorish-Americans are descendants of Moroccans and born in America. The Moorish Science Temple of America was founded for the purpose of uplifting fallen humanity. Noble Drew Ali began to uplift the Moorish-Americans by teaching them to be themselves.

This religion is known as Islamism. Islamism is an old religion. The Moorish flag is red with a five pointed green star in the center. The five points represent Love, Truth, Peace, Freedom, and Justice. The Moorish flag is over 10,000 years old. Friday is the Holy Day of the Moorish-Americans because it is the day on which man was formed in flesh and it was on a Friday when He departed out of flesh. Jesus was a Prophet of Allah. Jesus was born in Bethlehem of Judah in the House of David. Jesus' mother and father were Mary and Joseph. Some of the Great fathers through which Jesus came are Abraham, Boaz by Ruth, Jesse, King David, King Solomon, Hezekiah, and Joseph by Mary.

Allah sent Jesus to this earth to save the Israelites from the iron hand of oppression of the pale skinned nations of

Europe, who were governing a portion of Palestine at that time. That was about 2,000 years ago. Ruth was a Moabite. Moroccans is the modern name for Moabites.

The Moroccan Empire is located in Northwest Africa. This information was provided by *The Koran Questions for Moorish Americans.*

8

Thou Shalt Practice Good Hygiene

According to Webster's Collegiate Dictionary, hygiene is defined as the science concerned with maintenance of sound health and prevention of disease, and the conditions and practices that contribute to disease prevention.

Sound health and disease prevention are becoming major issues inside prison. There is a plethora of inmates that are sick before they come into the prison system. Then there are diseases that seem to be common in prison such as Hepatitis, MRSA, HIV, and AIDS. I used to live in a medical prison facility and I have witnessed many people succumbing to those diseases mentioned previously. Although I wasn't sick, I had to maintain my health through practicing god hygiene. I will elaborate on those diseases later on in chapter ten. My objective for this chapter is to provide you with different techniques that will prevent disease from entering your body. Don't be fooled into thinking that as long as you don't engage in risky sexual behavior you can't become ill.

THE TEN HYGIENE COMMANDMENTS

Rule #1: <u>Wash your hands before and after using the restroom.</u> Not washing your hands after using the restroom is probably the fastest way to spread bacteria. People who don't wash their hands leave traces of urine and feces on telephones, doorknobs, tables, and chairs. This is how MRSA (also known as staph infection) is spread throughout prison. The truth is that most inmates don't wash their hands after they use the restroom. I used to post memos on the restroom walls reminding people to wash their hands. Never shake anyone's hand in prison unless you are wearing latex gloves. Always greet other prisoners with a closed fist, (aka, a pound).

Some people will use the restroom and run water on their hands without using soap or hand sanitizer. This only helps to spread bacteria. Soaps have special chemical agents that destroy bacteria on contact. People basically have good and bad bacteria that cling to their hands. The good bacteria is needed to fight the bad bacteria. Soap destroys the bad bacteria, but if you use it too often you can destroy the good bacteria. This is similar to brushing your teeth too much and destroying the enamel on your teeth.

Rule #2: <u>Clean the shower before and after you use it.</u> Every prison has a bathroom janitor who cleans the shower once or twice daily. In between that time forty or fifty inmates may use a single shower without cleaning it one time. How would you feel of fifty people used the shower at your house without cleaning it and you were number fifty-one? That's exactly what happens in prison. Hair, soap, dirty boxers, soap wrappers, face towels, dirt and grime lay everywhere.

Imagine taking a shower in a dumpster. In some prison showers the drains get backed up with hair, dirt, and scum. That same hair, dirt, and scum rises over the drain and freely runs through the toes of that person taking a shower. These things can be avoided by cleaning the shower before and after use. When cleaning the shower allow ten minutes to elapse after you spray and rinse because you don't need to be around cleaning agents (chemicals) with open pores.

Rule #3: <u>Never share cigarettes</u>. Smoking cigarettes is harmful to your health. I could tell you why but you already know. If you smoke cigarettes then I advise you to stop. Never ask anyone to save you a piece of their cigarette. The saliva left on a cigarette is full of plaque and blood. Smoking behind someone can put abscesses and sores on your lips and mouth. What if the person who passes you the cigarette just used the restroom and didn't wash his/her hands? Now you are about to smoke a cigarette laced with plaque, blood, urine, and feces. Have you ever smelled a smoker's breath by accident? It's not a good scent. Harmful bacteria in someone's mouth can cause gum disease, tooth decay, and worst of all heart disease. Sharing cigarettes is a breeding ground for hepatitis, tuberculosis, and MRSA. Smoking alone is a filthy habit, but sharing cigarettes is even worse. If you smoke cigarettes I want you to put this book down and look in a mirror right now! It is really cool to walk around with an ash tray for a mouth? You are already hurting yourself by walking around with burned lips and yellow teeth. Tighten up!

Rule #4 <u>Never use silverware.</u> The silverware in the kitchens (forks, knives, and spoons) is constantly being used over and over again. I have talked to inmates that worked as dishwashers in prison and they admitted to not cleaning the silverware properly. One guy told me that on some nights he wouldn't wash the silverware at all. Don't be fooled into thinking the staff is concerned because most of them have their own silverware at home to be concerned with. The good thing is that it's not over. You can avoid using the silverware in the kitchen by using plastic disposable forks, knives, and spoons from the canteen or commissary.

Rule #5 <u>Never drink out of cups</u> for obvious reasons similar to rule four. You can use Styrofoam cups from the canteen or don't drink anything at all in the dining hall.

Rule #6 <u>Never wash your face with a face cloth.</u> Okay, you just got a bag of clean clothes from the clothes house. Inside the bag are five t-shirts, five boxers, five pairs of socks, two face cloths, and two towels. You decide to wash your face with one of the face cloths in your bag. The next step is to remove the face cloth from the bag and run some water while grabbing your face soap. Stop! Before you lather your face cloth with soap and place it on your face, ask yourself the following questions. How many other inmates have

used this face cloth that I'm about to put on my face?
Don't put any type of towel or cloth on your face. This
is how MRSA is spread. Wash your face with your
hands then let your face air dry.

Rule #7 <u>Get your clothes washed separately from
population.</u> When you get your clothes washed
separately from population this is called special
wash. There are two routes that you can take to
receive special wash. The first way is to fill out a sick
call form. A sick call form is a paper that a prisoner
fills out when he/she is sick. This form goes to the
medical staff. The nurse receives the sick call form
and if your sickness is kind of serious the nurse will
notify the doctor. If your sickness is not so serious
(like a loud cough) then the nurse will take care of
you him/herself. When you fill out your sick form
write that the laundry you are receiving is making
you itch and breaking your skin out in rashes. A few
days later you should be placed on special wash. You
will get brand new t-shirts, socks, boxers, towels, and
face cloths. These items are yours to keep. Whenever
they get dirty just take them to the clothes house and
someone will wash them and return them to you.
Make sure your name is on your laundry bag.

The second way to receive special wash is to pay the person
in charge of washing clothes a few dollars every week to
wash your clothes. I don't know how much the clothes
house man is going to charge you but two dollars a week
or per laundry bag seems reasonable. I prefer the second
was because my clothes always smell and look better when
I pay to have them washed. This way you can build a
business relationship with the clothes house man and

whenever he gets new sheets, blankets, or pillows you will be the first to receive them.

Rule #8 <u>Floss your teeth.</u> I can literally count on one hand the number of prisoners I have actually seen flossing their teeth during my prison term. Plaque gets in between your teeth. Plaque is leftover food that starts to rot in your mouth. If you don't floss your teeth the plaque (leftover food) in your mouth will get hard and dentists will have to scrape the plaque out with a very sharp object. This process is very painful and bloody. You can avoid this by purchasing a box of dental floss from your commissary or canteen. The most I ever paid for dental floss in prison was a dollar and thirty-two cents. Dental floss comes in two forms, waxed and non-waxed. The waxed form is for people with sensitive gums and teeth. Some dental floss even comes in mint flavor. Once you purchase the dental floss you should brush your teeth first. After you brush your teeth pull the thread from the box and wrap it around your index finger. Once you wrap it around your finger pull on the string some more until you have about a foot of string in front of you. Use the sharp metal object in the box to break the string. After you break the string wrap the loose end around your other index finger. Begin to place the thread in between your teeth and gums. Clean the excess food and plaque from in between your teeth using the dental floss. Spit the plaque out in the toilet. Don't spit in the sink or the trash can. Be sure to clean all your teeth and don't be surprised if you spit out a lot of blood. Don't swallow the food stuck in your teeth because this can cause stomach ulcers.

If you can't understand my method of flossing please ask the nurse or dentist to give you instructions. I was shocked at how many people in prison never floss. I once asked an older gentleman that I met in prison if he flossed his teeth. His reply was, "I only floss the teeth that I want to keep." Of course he still had all of his teeth.

Rule #9 <u>Never touch doorknobs or telephones.</u> By now you should have caught on to how these germs and bacteria are being spread. Now you have to be very strategic in the germ warfare. Doorknobs and telephones harbor more germs than the toilet. (That's not a joke.) When you get up in the morning grab a small pile of paper towels and put them in your back pocket. Whenever you approach a doorknob use one of the paper towels in your back pocket to open the door. You can throw the paper towel away once you reach your destination. Always clean phones off with disinfectant before usage. After you clean the phone off allow five minutes to elapse before using the phone so you won't have to breathe harsh chemicals. Use a paper towel or napkin to hold the phone while talking. You may not always remember to do this but in time it will become a good habit. When people talk on the phone they leave dirt, feces, skin, blood, and saliva on the phone. People might look at you funny when you start practicing good hygiene but it is better to be safe than sorry.

Rule #10 <u>Cover your head when you sleep</u>. I used to use one of my t-shirts to cover my head at night. The other inmate would laugh at me and call me an Arab. They couldn't understand why I would cover my head before I went to sleep. People cough, sneeze, and pass gas when they are asleep. If you are lying near someone when he/she sneezes then you can catch whatever germ is airborne at the time. I cover my head and face to block out germs. Bugs also play a major part in my decision. When you go to sleep with your head and face uncovered you leave yourself open for spiders, roaches, flies, or any pestilence to crawl in your ears and/or nose. Some prisoners work outside during the day cutting grass and picking up trash. When they return to the prison facility they bring tics, leeches, worms, and parasites with them. Some of these guys don't wash their bodies properly and bugs crawl off of them and on other inmates.

I was once sitting in the dining hall in prison back in 2004 when a man sitting across from me actually had an army or ants running from his shirt sleeve to my tray. I had just taken the first bite of my food when I noticed the tiny army of ants heading towards my tray. I jumped from the table and informed the man of the ant farm coming from his shirt sleeve. He just wiped the ants from the table and continued to eat. That was hardcore. I never reached that level in prison.

Follow these rules and things will be a little better for you. Many people die in prison because they don't practice good hygiene. Stay healthy and live long. Don't forget to pass these rules along to others.

9

Thou Shalt Not Be A Dummy (Education)

Knowledge is power and every experience that you go through should be viewed as self education. Right now you are being educated on the consequences of breaking the law. Hopefully you will share your experience with someone else so he/she won't have to travel in the same direction.

You can take advantage of your time by educating yourself. Your main purpose for education is to improve your quality of lifestyle. This can only be done by changing the way you think. You can change the way you think by studying new thinking strategies. This is the first step to education. It was very hard for me to admit that some of my values were poor.

I had received my education from the streets. You know, the hard knocks life. I used to be proud of myself because I knew enough to survive the streets. One day a strange thing happened. I didn't want to be in the streets anymore. I wanted to live a normal life. A wife, kids, and a dog didn't sound like a bad idea. The problem was that all I knew was the streets. I didn't realize that I needed to learn how to obtain the things I wanted. I thought that as long as I made some money then all of the things that I desired would come to me naturally. Oh what a tangle web we weave. I became frustrated because my street education was not effective when I tried to apply it to a family situation. My plan of living a normal life had failed and the end result was prison. No, I didn't hurt anyone in my family, but the fact that my plan had failed pulled me back into the streets. I wasn't ready to accept that it takes more than street knowledge to live a normal life and raise a decent family. No, I believed that everything I learned on the streets could be applied to everything in life. I thought that I could make the people in my family do exactly what I tell them like I did people on the streets. It was like trying to fit a square peg into a circle. It just wouldn't fit and this was all due to my ignorance.

You wouldn't visit China and start speaking French. It wouldn't matter if you could speak French fluently, it just doesn't fit in China. This is a form of ignorance that might be holding you back from living a quality lifestyle. One of the hardest things I had to do was admit that I had been taught some things that were detrimental to my well being. If you decide to become a music producer then you will need to study the music industry. Selling weed and carrying a gun cannot teach you about the music industry.

Whatever you want to do in life will require education in that field of practice. I don't want to make this chapter complicated for you. Whatever you want to do in life has a blueprint, whether it requires school or your own research.

All I can do is provide you with a few tips on how you can educate yourself in prison.

A positive mental attitude (pma) is the first step to educating yourself. Go to the library and read all the self help books you can get your hands on. These books have excellent strategies that will give you a new sense of awareness and raise your self esteem. Your success depends on your attitude and positive influence on the people around you. Some prisoners become bitter when they get locked up and their attitudes are very negative and harmful to themselves and people around them. These people are usually labeled idiots, jerks, or even worse. Self-education for someone who is bitter is highly unlikely to occur. That's why a positive mental attitude is the first step to improvement.

The second step to education yourself is self-awareness classes. Most state prisons will offer some type of curriculum for self-awareness. You have to check with your case programmer to find out what classes are available to you. One class that may be available to you is Alcoholics Anonymous. This class offers a twelve step program to help overcome alcohol addiction. Narcotics Anonymous is a class that offers a twelve step program to help overcome drug addiction. Character Education is a class that will help build strong ethical and moral values. Cognitive Behavior is a class that will help you exercise good judgment when making critical decisions. Human Resource Management is a class that will teach you how to plan for a successful future. A G.E.D. class provides a standard high school equivalency test to help one obtain his/her high school diploma. The Re-entry program prepares inmates for life outside of prison. Teachers show students how to fill out job applications, prepare professional resumes, and how to have successful job interviews. Independent study is a program that contains college courses such as Business Management and Paralegal Studies. Anyone who joins this program will have to mail their homework into the college that he/she is assigned to. Textbooks will be provided for study. College credits will be given if the course is completed in satisfactory condition.

Stay focused! Your life has gone downhill if you are in prison. All you can do is climb back up the hill. You can do this by planning your future now. Read books that will show you how to get the most out of life. I have unfortunately seen hundreds of prisoners waste valuable time watching television, playing board games, reading fiction books, or staring into space. If you ever see a person constantly staring into space and doing nothing else be very cautious of him/her. An idle mind is the devil's workshop. Sometimes people get stuck on events that happened in the past and they find it difficult to move on. If this sounds like you then I would advise you to talk to your counselor. Your counselor can decide if you need professional help.

The third step is deciding what you are going to do with the rest of your life. How can you be a better? What kind of career would help you and your family during these tough economic times? What kind of jobs do you find exciting? Put this book down right now and write down everything you want to do in life. Maybe you want to be a lawyer or a racecar driver. Whatever the case may be, you need to start studying to find out how you can reinvent yourself. Only you can make a difference in your life.

I once heard a very wise man say, "Whatever you do in life, make sure you are the best who ever done it." That wise man was Donald Trump. As you probably know, Mr. Trump is the perfect example of the best to ever do it. I don't care if you want to paint houses for a living. Learn how to paint. Learn what kind of paint is used on houses. Find out if there is a market for house painters in your area. Check to see what kind of license a painter needs to paint houses. Find out if you are eligible for a loan to purchase painting supplies. Call home and ask someone in your family to go online for information. Have your family member mail you that info if you don't have internet access. Become an expert in whatever career you choose. If you are not sure about what type of career you would like to pursue ask your programmer to sing your name up for a vocational test. A vocational test will show you what type of career would best suit you. More than likely you will have five or six professions that you might be good at so choose wisely. Have fun!

Always have a dictionary around so that you can search for words that are unfamiliar to you. Owning a dictionary is mandatory. If you use profanity a dictionary can enhance your vocabulary tremendously to the point where curse words won't be a part of your vocabulary. Create a vocabulary notebook or folder by writing five words and their meanings inside of the notebook every day.

Please don't think that you have to study twenty-four hours a day. Take a break sometimes. You have to rest your eyes and brain when you study. It's always good to let new discoveries gradually sink into your brain. Too much information at one time can lead to confusion and chaos. Go ahead and take a few days off. Those books will be there when you decide to study again.

Use your time away from your studies to socialize with people, read fiction books, play board games, or watch television. Don't isolate yourself from population too much because you might attract negative attention from a negative person. He/she may try to close in on you during long bouts of isolation. You can confuse the undesirable by mixing it up. Never have a set pattern of operations in prison. If you study Monday through Thursday one week, then switch it up and study Thursday through Sunday the next week. Create a network of friends so that undesirables know that others are concerned about your well being.

Block out loud noise when you study. You can accomplish this by listening to earphones of wearing earplugs. Either way you will have to learn how to stay focused because noise in prison will always be around.

Be aware of that jealous inmate who hates to see you doing something positive like reading and learning. He/she is the person that always wants to engage in a conversation whenever they see you studying. This person will disguise him/herself as a friend but their objective is to take you away from educating yourself. They want to humiliate you because they are miserable and misery loves company. This person is known as the wannabee (refer to chapter 2). When the wannabee approaches you simply tell him/her that you are busy.

Keep up on current events. Read the newspaper and up to date magazines like Popular Science. You don't have to become a Shaolin monk just because you are in prison. Find out what's happening in the community you live in. If you are far away from home one of your relatives can order the local newspaper in your area and have it sent to you. Check with the mail clerk at the prison facility that you are in. These current events affect the lives of prisoners and civilians. You may be studying a career that is failing in these tough economic times. The newspaper and certain magazines can tell you what businesses are thriving and which ones are failing. I know your resources for information are limited so you have to work with what you got.

If you have poor eyesight you should take at least two days off a week from reading, because when you read a lot you are straining your eyes. Give your eyes time to relax. Try not to read until the words in front of you become blurry. If this happens then you are putting too much of a strain on your eyes.

Get into the habit of sharing information with other inmates. Don't be stingy with the knowledge you acquire when studying. Pass books along to other individuals who are serious about educating themselves. Some inmates are holding tons of literature that can benefit you greatly. These people have been down for years and they have a great deal of knowledge. They are willing to share the things that they have learned, but they have a don't ask-don't tell policy. That means if you don't ask them about the books they are holding then they won't tell you about them. This is why you have to create a social network with people.

I have had the pleasure of meeting some of the most gifted and intelligent people in state prison. You will see what I am writing about once you start networking with others. Make the best out of your resources. Study different subjects the same way you did in school. In doing so you will become what some people call a well rounded individual. You will be able to hold intelligent conversations with the best of them.

Always remember to seek God first in whatever you do. (Refer the Chapter 7). Your spiritual well being is the most important being. Educate yourself with God's words and everything else will fall in order.

10

Thou Shalt Not Get Sick
(Infections and Disease)

There are a number of diseases that plague the prison system. I wrote this chapter to give you the information about these diseases so that you may recognize the symptoms. Remember to get an annual checkup from the doctor at your facility. Always pay close attention to your body and look for signs or symptoms of sickness.

Some diseases don't have visible symptoms so you need to rely on your doctor's expertise. Diet and nutrition are major factors concerning your health (refer to Chapter 6). If you have a chronic disease, don't give up because the medicines of today can calm the effects of any sickness you may have. Medical technology is improving every day. There have been tremendous breakthroughs with chronic diseases within the last ten years.

Illness can be caused by a number of external forces called agents such as microorganisms (bacteria), toxic substances (poison), even electricity. Stress is a well known factor influencing high blood pressure and heart attacks. Malnutrition can cause disease along with pollution and poverty. Here is a profile of the major diseases to be aware of in prison.

HIV/AIDS – HIV is caused by a virus that you can get from other people. There is a breakdown of the body's defense system, called the immune system, and this breakdown produces a susceptibility to certain diseases. Often there is a specific cluster of disorders and symptoms associated with HIV, a syndrome.

Scientists are also studying the possibility of cofactors, such as other biological, psychological, and social factors, and substances such as drugs or alcohol, which may affect each individual's response to HIV infection and the course of the illness.

The FIRST important thing to know about the HIV virus is that it picks as its host your immune system, the very defenders of your body against all disease. In particular it goes into the T4 cells, which coordinate the immune system. This means that the entire defense system is going to be demobilized. So when any harmful microorganisms of any kind begin multiplying in you body, there isn't a strong defense system to fight them off because the HIV virus has weakened the defense system. When HIV first enters your body you still have a strong defense system. The over time you lose some of your defenders and you get a little sick because you are susceptible to infection. With more time and without treatment you will usually get sicker and sicker because your defense system can't function.

Technically no one dies from HIV. They die from one or more of the infections that took advantage of a weak immune system.

Another special characteristic of the HIV virus is that it replicates very fast, twenty times faster than the average flu virus. This means that the number of viruses increases rapidly. Also the virus tends to have a relatively fast rate of binding to its host cell targets compared to the rate of binding between antibodies and the virus.

One of the most significant characteristics of the HIV virus is how great a mutation rate it has. A mutation is a mistake that happens in the blueprint when it is printed. Although mutants are rarely stronger that the original organisms and many of them die, some of them survive and in time they may become new strains of the virus.

One part of the blueprint for the HIV virus tends to mutate a great deal, namely the part that designs the protein coat. Since the human immune system, including the antibodies, recognizes viral invaders by their protein coats, new mutants may be able to hide from the human immune system gaining time to replicate and infect more host cells.

Although the T4 cell seems to be the main host cell attacked by the HIV virus, other types of cells also serve as hosts. These include T8 (helper) cells, the macrophage, some brain cells, and possibly cells in the liver. Other possibilities are also being studied.

The HIV virus, like any virus, has a protein coat. It has particular chemicals that attract it to the protein coat of the particular host cell.

HIV is found in semen. Semen transmits the virus between a man and a woman and between two men during sex. HIV is found in blood. Blood can transmit the virus during sex. HIV is found in vaginal/cervical secretions, and these secretions can transmit the virus from a woman to a man or between two women during sex.

HIV appears to be less concentrated in vaginal/cervical secretions than in semen and blood. The danger of transmission increases when a man or a woman has another sexually transmitted disease, because sores are a place of entry for the virus. The danger of transmission increases when a woman has a vaginal infection because of the greater number of white blood cells in the vaginal area. White blood cells carry HIV.

Menstrual blood, like all blood, carries HIV and can transmit HIV. Some individuals with HIV infection have HIV in their saliva. It is in very low concentration. There are no known cases of transmission of HIV via saliva, but scientists at this time cannot say with absolute certainty that saliva can't transmit HIV. It is theoretically possible, although very low risk. Blood in saliva increases the risk of transmission of HIV.

In the United States there are fewer documented cases of transmission from a woman to a man than from a man to a woman. But in Africa woman to man transmission is almost equal to man to woman transmission.

The HIV antibody test looks for the presence of antibodies to the HIV virus in the blood. If an individual tests positive it means that antibodies to the HIV virus are present in the person's blood. If antibodies are present it must be assumed that the person has been infected with the HIV virus and is capable of infecting others. A positive HIV antibody test does not necessarily mean that the individual will develop AIDS.

Reports now show however that the vast majority

of people infected with HIV will eventually progress to AIDS.

A positive test result to the HIV antibody test means that the HIV antibodies are present in the person's blood. It also means that it can be assumed that the person has been infected with HIV. The person is capable of infecting other people with HIV through unsafe activities.

Some people with HIV eventually develop AIDS. Testing for HIV antibodies cannot tell about the state of an individual's health either now or in the future. A person who is HIV positive should:

- Eat well, avoid stress, and seek medical help
- Seek counseling prior to becoming pregnant
- Avoid donating blood, sperm, and organs
- Practice safe sex.

A negative test result means that the antibody to HIV is absent. This means either the person has not been infected with HIV of the person has been infected with HIV but his/her body has not yet produced antibodies.

The information on HIV was provided through the members of the ACE program (AIDS Counseling and Education) of the Bedford Hills Correctional Facility. ACE's book is titled 'Breaking the Walls of Silence.'

<u>Hepatitis A</u>- Hepatitis A is spread from person to person by poor personal hygiene or when water or food is contaminated by sewage. The disease is very common in developing countries with inadequate systems of sanitation. The early symptoms of the disease are similar to other viral infections, with muscle and joint aching, fever, headache, and weakness. But the most prominent symptoms are loss of appetite and nausea.

In some cases the illness disappears with no further symptoms or signs, but more often jaundice develops after a few days. Usually the hepatitis clears up without treatment in 2 to 8 weeks.

<u>Hepatitis B and C</u>- Hepatitis B and C spread from person to person by two main routes; contact with infected blood and heterosexual or homosexual activities. Outbreaks caused by contaminated water supplies have been reported on rare occasions. Until the mid-1980's these forms of hepatitis were commonly transmitted by blood transfusion and by treatment of patients with blood products (such as factor VIII for hemophilia), but this risk has now been almost eliminated by testing of blood donors and the use of genetic engineering to make safe blood products.

Infection still occurs commonly, however, among drug addicts who share needles, and it may be transmitted by tattooists and acupuncturists who fail to sterilize their equipment.

Hepatitis B and C are also an occupational risk for physicians, nurses, and health care workers who come into frequent contact with blood. Hepatitis B (and to a lesser extent, hepatitis C) is a common sexually transmitted disease, and along with other such diseases occurs frequently in prostitutes and in male homosexuals with many partners. Hepatitis B, and probably hepatitis C, may be transmitted from a pregnant woman to her fetus; this is a serious problem in developing countries.

The blood of someone infected with either hepatitis B or C is highly infectious both during the incubation period (6 to 12 weeks, sometimes longer, between the time you are infected and the time the symptoms appear) and after the illness has seemingly cleared up. Some people become lifelong carriers of these viruses.

The risk of progressive, life threatening, chronic active hepatitis is greater in those infected with hepatitis B and C, and they are also more likely to develop chronic liver disease eventually.

Blood banks now routinely use screening tests for the two types of hepatitis transmitted by blood, and the risk of contracting hepatitis from a blood transfusion is declining. A vaccine against hepatitis B is available for people at high risk, such as physicians and nurses. Hepatitis A remains a risk for people travelling to remote areas of developing countries.

A blood test can be done to determine whether you are immune. If you are not, immunization with gamma-globulin gives protection from hepatitis A for a few months.

<u>Acute Hepatitis</u>- Acute hepatitis is a sudden inflammation of the liver caused by one of several viruses, including the three viruses called A,B, and C, but a few attacks of hepatitis seem to be caused by yet other viruses. The viruses cause diseases with many characteristics in common, such as jaundice, pale stools, dark urine, loss of energy, loss of appetite, and fever. However there are also substantial differences in the way the diseases are transmitted and their outlook.

If your physician suspects that you have virus hepatitis, he or she will ask you about risk factors, examine you, and then take a blood sample for laboratory testing. It is important to determine which virus is responsible, and the extent of the damage to the function of your liver to evaluate the potential severity of the illness. Blood tests may be repeated at regular intervals to monitor any damage to the liver to help reduce the risk of getting hepatitis through sexual contact.

Until you hear the results of your blood tests you will not know which hepatitis virus is responsible, and you should assume that your stool and all your body fluids are infectious. If you are recovering at home you should flush stools from any bedpan use directly down the toilet, sterilize the bedpan, and wash your hands scrupulously. An infected person may, however, share a bathroom with the rest of the family. Any soiled clothing or linen should be laundered in hot water with a detergent and bleach. Toilets and floors should be cleaned thoroughly and often with hot water and a disinfectant.

If your symptoms are mild your physician will probably recommend that you stay home for several weeks, eat a high protein, high carbohydrate diet, and get plenty of rest.

Chronic hepatitis- Anyone who has had an attack of acute hepatitis may develop chronic hepatitis. The risk appears to be highest with hepatitis C, with up to 50% of those who have the acute form developing chronic hepatitis. It may be caused by other less common causes of liver inflammation or by reactions to drugs including isoniazid, which is used to treat tuberculosis.

Chronic hepatitis is classified into two main types, chronic persistent hepatitis and chronic active hepatitis. In both diseases the body responds with an immune response that may damage the cells in the liver. In chronic persistent hepatitis progression of the illness is slow, and the patient usually remains in good health and is unlikely to develop cirrhosis.

Chronic active hepatitis is a less predictable disease. In a number of cases there is a steady, progressive destruction of liver cells that leads to cirrhosis. In some people the disease comes and goes at times in response to treatment. In other cases, however, the disease responds well to treatment and the symptoms of the disease clear up.

The severity of chronic hepatitis varies from case to case. Some people have no symptoms of the disease for long periods but occasionally have episodes of jaundice, joint pain, nausea, fever, and loss of appetite. Uncommonly, people with chronic hepatitis B may have acute flare-ups caused by yet another virus, the Delta virus, which affects only those already infected with hepatitis B. Others have no symptoms despite having mild liver inflammation for many years.

<u>Staphylococcal infections</u>- Staphylococcal infections (also known as staph or MRSA) normally live in the nose, mouth, rectum, or genital area without causing any kind of infection. However, when an injury such as a puncture wound introduces the organism into some other part of the body, the staph bacteria can create toxic substances that tunnel into tissues, destroying and dissolving matter along the way.

The bacteria can produce pus-containing abscesses anywhere on or in the body. If you have an illness such as chronic liver or kidney disease, diabetes, or cancer you are particularly susceptible to infection by staph bacteria.

Several fairly common skin infections can be caused by staph bacteria. Boils, impetigo, cellulitis, and paronychia (which affects the nails) are examples. Staph bacteria can infect any open cut or wound on the skin.

The staph infection is a smaller version of a boil.

Small, white-headed pimples erupt around hair follicles anywhere on the body. Friction, blockage of the follicle, or injury (such as a cut from shaving) can cause a rash-like eruption.

Toxic-shock syndrome is caused by a staph infection somewhere in the body releasing a toxin into the bloodstream that causes fever, diarrhea, and a sunburn-like rash that leads eventually to skin peeling. Toxic-shock syndrome was widely publicized in the early 1980's because of an epidemic associated with staph infections caused by using super-absorbent tampons. Toxic-shock syndrome may also occur less commonly along with infected wounds, surgery, or other staph infections.

The full blown syndrome may lead to profound lowering of blood pressure and damage to the liver, kidneys, and other organs. It can be fatal if not treated promptly.

Any skin wounds, whether they are caused by an injury or made during surgery, can be complicated by infections caused by staph bacteria ordinarily found on the skin. Symptoms and signs are the oozing pus, pain, redness, heat and fever, and chills.

Staph bacteria can infect any part of your body. In the eye it can cause sties, some types of conjunctivitis, and orbital cellulitis. In the breasts they can cause breast abscesses, particularly in nursing mothers.

Staph infections may develop in bones and joints from bacteria that spread through the bloodstream. As the organism circulates in the bloodstream it tends to lodge in the long bones of the arms and legs, or somewhere in the vertebrae. In the lungs staph pneumonia can develop into pneumonia. This type of pneumonia may occur if the bacteria circulate in the bloodstream, if an abscess lodges onto one of the valves on the right side of the heart, or along with influenza.

If staff infects the inner lining of the heart endocarditis will develop. This disorder can cause irreversible heart damage and is fatal in some cases.

Staph food poisoning with cramps, vomiting and diarrhea can occur if you eat food that contains toxins produced by the bacteria.

Staph infrequently causes a colon infection if you take an antibiotic medication that kills many kinds of bacteria, including those that normally live in the digestive tract. This may upset the balance of microorganisms in the intestines so that the staph then over multiply and cause abdominal pain, a swollen abdomen, and bloody diarrhea.

In mild cases of staph infection such as folliculitis or boils, cleaning the infected area with soap and water and eliminating the cause of infections often clears up the problem. If the infection persists despite self-help treatment, or if you have severe symptoms, see your physician. He or she will probably prescribe an antibiotic to fight the infection.

<u>Streptococcal sore throat</u>- Streptococcal sore throat is also called strep throat. It is impossible to distinguish between a sore throat caused by an infection with streptococcus pyogenes (strep throat) from that caused by a viral infection without seeing a physician. Both the bacterial and viral infections are common in childhood between the ages of five and fifteen.

If the tonsils are substantially enlarged and fiery red strep throat is likely. To determine if you have strep throat your physician will take a sample of secretions from your throat (a throat culture) for laboratory analysis. An 'instant' strep test, taken in the physician's office, can produce results in as few as ten to thirty minutes. If you do not have strep throat you may have a virus infection.

Initial symptoms of virus infections mimic those of a cold, such as runny nose and watery eyes. The information on the diseases such as hepatitis, staph infection, and strep throat was provided by the American Medical Association Family Medical Guide, Third Edition.

Bonus Chapters

11

Thou Shalt Not Grieve Too Long

This chapter is a very sensitive one because dealing with the death of a loved one while you are incarcerated can be very complicated. In some cases the prison administration will allow an inmate to attend the funeral of a loved one as long as the deceased is considered to be the inmate's immediate family (mother, father, husband, wife, sister, brother, or child). Some prison administrations will deny an inmate the right to attend the funeral of a loved one if the deceased is in another state.

Family support is often next to non-existent for a prisoner when dealing with death. Most inmates will have a few associates in prison who will be sympathetic to a family member dying. Prison is not a place where you want to become emotional. You have sharks in prison who prey on people's emotions. This is where the problem presents itself. In your time of grieving for a loved one a few phony associates will offer their condolences but it will always be with evil intentions.

Never be surprised at how petty the guy sleeping next to you can be. Some will even offer words of inspiration but they expect to be compensated for it later on. You have to find inner strength during this time (Refer to Chapter 7). The truth is that death is irreversible and something you can't change. You have to keep yourself together and continue to move on. Your falling apart won't bring that loved one back to life. More than likely your deceased relative wouldn't want you to lose your mind over his/her death. This is the time that we need to show strength and courage.

If you can't attend the funeral it might be wise to express your support to the rest of your family through letters, phone calls, and visits. Send cards and/or poems.

Having a loved one return to the essence while you are incarcerated is way too common. Before I wrote this chapter I asked twenty prisoners if they had a loved one die during his/her incarceration. Surprisingly, sixteen out of twenty answered yes. If you have five years or more on your prison sentence then it is probably safe to say that you will lose a family member during your prison sentence. Unfortunately I lost four family members during my incarceration. I took my frustrations out on the weight pile. I noticed that every time I worked out I felt better about dealing with the deaths in my family.

If you have a friend or associate who is dealing with the death of a family member please remember to give him/her space. Allow him/her enough time to get through the whole ordeal. Some people become very emotional after a few weeks or months when dealing with death. You have to watch your friends carefully when they are dealing with the loss of a family member. I have witnessed my friend literally go insane after losing a loved one. It wasn't instant insanity, but more like a silent insanity over a period of time. He would do things that were way out of his character like have homosexual relations with other inmates who were suspected to be carrying HIV. I once heard him talking about raping a nurse. I had to stop dealing with him because he had lost his sanity over the death of a loved one. Pay close attention to your surroundings. Never get carried away with laughing and joking with people because you never know who might have just received the news of a death in his/her family. If you are dealing with the death of a loved one and you feel overwhelmed with sorrow and hopelessness then I would advise you to seek professional help. I kept this chapter short because if you're going through this situation I want you to get over it and keep it moving. God bless you and your family!

12

Thou Shalt Remain Calm
(Pre release Anxiety)

Pre-release anxiety attacks every inmate within his/her last nine months before release. The symptoms of pre-release anxiety are stress, insomnia, overeating, and becoming easily irritated with others. The root or pre-release anxiety is fear. After doing years behind the iron curtain the thought of being released into the world brings fear of the unknown. You don't know what is going to happen once you are released. Sure you have a plan for success. I understand that failure is not an option for you, but the reality is that you still don't know what is going to happen until you get out. People and plans change sometimes, and you know this and the anxiety can be overbearing at times.

You have to be very cautious during this time because your good temperament towards others can easily change to bad. Pre-release anxiety can cause you to talk to people in harsh tones. I have witnessed incidents of violence due to one's pre-release anxiety. If you get into a fight in prison you can be charged with assault and sentenced to more time. This has happened to a number of people who were about to be released. Don't fall into that trap because doing extra time is definitely not part of the plan.

I'm quite sure you noticed a prisoner's behavior change when he/she was about to be released. Some become very loud and obnoxious and some become introverted and withdrawn. This is what pre-release anxiety does to people. Most of the time a person suffering from pre-release anxiety will think that everyone around him/her is acting strange because people will pick up on the sufferer's weird behavior and decide to give that person a little space. If you are about to be released and your friends and associates seem to have become a little distant it may be that you are showing symptoms of pre-release anxiety. Sometimes people will distance themselves from you even if you don't show them symptoms of pre-release anxiety, because others before you have shown them symptoms of pre-release anxiety so they are playing it safe with you just in case you start acting like a donkey.

Imagine yourself as a racetrack for horses and the horses are about to line up for the race. Five minutes before the race the horses are calm but as soon as they line up at the gate for the start of the race they begin to buck up. The jockey has to work hard in order to keep the horse calm but the horse knows that when the gate opens it is time to take off. This is pre-release anxiety. That is why your friends or associates may distance themselves from you when you are about to be released. Would you stand around a horse who is about to be let out of the gate at a race?

Never take it personally if this happens to you and